THE FAMILY BUSINESS MANIFESTO

THE FAMILY BUSINESS MANIFESTO

A ROADMAP TO **PEACE** IN THE FAMILY AND **PROSPERITY** IN THE BUSINESS

MICHAEL MIRAU

LIONCREST
PUBLISHING

THE FAMILY BUSINESS MANIFESTO
A Roadmap to Peace in the Family and Prosperity in the Business

FIRST EDITION

ISBN 978-1-5445-4604-9 *Paperback*
978-1-5445-4603-2 *Ebook*

To God, for the amazing life I have been given. I am a blessed man.

And to my mom and dad. It is from them that I saw the positive power and impact a family business can have on our family. I learned so much!

CONTENTS

FAMILY BUSINESS MANIFESTO

A MANIFESTO IS A STATEMENT OF YOUR BELIEFS. THIS IS my manifesto about family business.

Ten-point family business manifesto:

1. Family businesses are the cornerstone of the American economy and society.
2. Family businesses create an opportunity to gain wealth and keep it in the family faster and easier than any other vehicle.
3. Family businesses have a unique set of challenges that make them different from a traditional business with owners and employees.
4. Family businesses provide an opportunity for the founders to develop and maintain their legacy for generations.
5. There are a set of principles that help family businesses have success and maintain healthy family relationships.
6. Assumptions add fuel to the fire in a family business.

7. Successful family businesses have clarity around roles and responsibilities.
8. Family businesses must be careful about ascribing motives to family behaviors.
9. Family is more important than the business.
10. Grace and peace in the family business are possible if we operate in love.

INTRODUCTION

I GREW UP IN A FAMILY BUSINESS. AS A CHILD, I SAW FIRST-hand what made a family business work and what challenges could hold it back. It would be many years, though, before I fully understood just how difficult it is to not just work in a family business but to found it, build it, and run it with family.

These days, as a business coach, I see the wins and losses many family businesses face daily. What I have not seen, however, is a definitive guide to how to run a family business successfully. A family business requires more from a founder than the average new business. You have to master the fundamentals of business while also developing systems and skills to navigate far more complex relationships. For some reason, though, no one is talking about this.

That is what this book is for. It is an opportunity to share the knowledge and insights I have gained over twenty-four years of working with organizations to help them become healthy and scalable. If you need this book, you are not alone. There are far more family businesses than you realize that are struggling with either the family side, the business side, or both in their company. Just consider the struggles one of my clients, Peter, was dealing with.

Peter (whose name, like all the others in this book, has been changed to protect their anonymity) was the successful founder of his family and family business. Through years of hard work and business savvy, he and his wife, Susan, had managed to build up several companies, all with the aim of sharing that success with their four children—Eric, Jessica, Zach, and Sam.

As their kids reached adulthood, it looked at first as if Peter might be able to see that dream become reality. The family business was bringing in several million in revenue. All the various companies were growing steadily, and there were opportunities for all the children to do their part. But somewhere along the line, it all started to go wrong.

The problems started with Jessica. As the only girl, she had a chip on her shoulder. From her perspective, she had never been given the same amount of attention or the same opportunities as her brothers. When Peter found out that she and her husband, Rich, were really focusing their efforts on their own startup business, he confronted her. That was the excuse she was looking for to exit the company entirely.

Once she was out of the office, she focused all her bitterness on her father. She put effort into convincing her brothers that Peter was selfish and at fault for promises he supposedly did not keep. Unfortunately, his sons were more than willing to agree.

That would have been bad enough, but Peter's sons were also having issues with one another. Eric, as the oldest, had always been the "perfect" one. He'd gone to college and studied business, entered the company immediately, and risen steadily to COO. When his father retired, he expected to take over the company.

Zach, the middle son, was his exact opposite. He was the prodigal child of the family. He didn't finish college and couldn't seem to hold down a job. When he finally came to them for work, Peter and Susan found themselves in a difficult position. They could either support him financially and risk him giving up on work entirely, support him through a job in the company and risk damage to the business, or refuse him both and risk him failing entirely. Considering their options, they felt a job in the family business was the least bad option. They gave him the title of VP of Special Projects—a position that was nothing more than a title and a paycheck.

This created a lot of resentment from Eric, who felt he had to carry all the weight for his younger brother. After Zach failed to show up for a meeting for the fourth week in a row, he tried to kick Zach out of the company entirely. That led to Zach kicking up a fuss to Peter and Susan. When Peter asked Eric to back down, Eric nearly quit.

Perhaps understandably, the youngest member of the family, Sam, wanted nothing to do with any of these dynamics. Quieter than the rest of the family, he was in charge of the plumbing company and ran it competently. But he resented any time he was pulled away from his work to deal with family issues or the broader business. Like Jessica, whom he was close to, he suffered from a victim mentality, seeing his older brothers and his parents as almost in a conspiracy against him. He didn't trust his brothers—either their actions or their judgment.

When Peter came to me, he was at the end of his rope. He had no idea what he should do with any of his children. None of them were on good terms with each other or with him, and their poor relationships were affecting his home life and his company.

"I'm heartbroken that we have this poison in our family," he told me.

When I asked him what he thought had caused all these problems, his answer was equally heartbreaking.

Lowering his eyes, he said, "My lack of attention when I brought them into the business."

Peter had done so much right in his family and his business life. But this one mistake was ruining both for him. While his motives were pure, the execution of his plan failed.

SO MUCH PROMISE, SO MUCH RISK

The issues faced by Peter and his family are not uncommon. In my role as a business coach, I see similar circumstances every day. But you don't have to be a business coach to understand the risk of mixing family and business. This is a story as old as time.

If you want to see evidence, open the Bible and look at the story of Jacob and Esau fighting over their father's blessing. Or flip ahead to see the arguments between Saul and his son Jonathan. The entire books of 1 Kings and 2 Kings are a continuous story of fathers who fail their sons and sons who refuse to follow the righteous lead of their fathers. The very idea of a prodigal son comes from a parable of Jesus about a wealthy farmer and his two sons—sons who were not so different from Eric and Zach.

Or, if you prefer, pick up a copy of the collected works of William Shakespeare and page through plays like *Hamlet*, *Richard III*, or *King Lear*, all of which are really about families broken by power and money.

This is a story we're still telling. The popular HBO Max show *Succession* was much loved by critics and fans in part because of the extremes of the behavior from the Roy family as they vied for control of their media empire.

These stories are so popular partly because they are so dramatic, but the drama is not exaggerated. After decades coaching family businesses, I can tell you that the extremes of *Succession*, Shakespeare, and the Bible are pretty accurate depictions of how family business can go wrong. They reflect relationships and interactions I see in every kind of family business, in every industry imaginable. It doesn't have to be an ancient farm, a medieval kingdom, or a multibillion-dollar entertainment organization to create the circumstances for such drama. These same issues play out at mom-and-pop shops on Main Street, USA, all the time.

I would argue that it's the duty of every founder to do all he or she can to reduce the possibility that their family business becomes another one of those tragic stories.

That's what we're going to cover in this book. This is a book for the founders out there who own their family business and want to steer both family and business to peace and prosperity. I'll use that term, founder, throughout this book, but I want to be clear from the outset that the term describes a position that anyone in the family could hold. A founder might be the father or the mother. It could also be a son or daughter. It could be a son- or daughter-in-law. The position refers to the person with the majority of the power and responsibility within their family and their family business.

In my experience, there is almost always one person who calls most of the shots in both. If that describes you, this book is for you.

I wrote this book for you because I love and admire family and family business. The family business can offer wonderful benefits to individuals, families, and communities. I own a family business myself.

I don't want to give a false impression here that family businesses are all doomed to failure. When you get it right, there's nothing more powerful than combining the family with business. After all, you're dealing with the people you should be able to trust more than anyone else in the world. You should know them better than anyone. They should have similar values. Families are meant to love one another, and there should be a desire to take care of one another. And at the same time, the whole family can benefit from their shared efforts. If everyone works hard for the family business, the results come more quickly than when a single person tries to do everything—and everyone gets to enjoy the fruits of that collective work.

That's not all, either. A family business can represent a wonderful inheritance. When run well, it can be a gift to future generations. You can think of it almost as a long-term annuity. Each generation can decide whether to work in the company and secure stability throughout their lives, or to sell the company to fund their dreams.

That's a kind of financial freedom that is very rare in this world.

But these institutions also come with immense risk, and we have to recognize that they bring extra challenges beyond a normal business. You may have noticed above that I qualified many of the benefits of family business. You *should* be able to trust family. Family *is meant to* look out for one another. A family business *can* represent a wonderful inheritance.

We all know that these hypothetical benefits don't always match reality. Families often have a lot of internal issues, and business has a way of exacerbating those problems.

When you add money and stress to any situation, it can make it worse. And this can happen whether a family business is extremely successful or struggling. If a founder isn't careful, success can create an entitlement mindset that runs through the whole family. You may have had to work hard to get where you are, but your children—and sometimes your cousins, siblings, or even spouse—may have become accustomed to money and success.

Your family may feel they are owed it without having to put the work in. When they don't get what they feel is owed, that can supercharge resentments. And it's no exaggeration to say that resentment can destroy a business and a family.

That isn't all, either. Family businesses can be rife with jealousy, suspicion, neglect, and mind games. Trust, the very quality that can be a family business's superpower, can be warped into distrust about every decision.

There's a reason that, according to familybusinesscenter.com, the average lifespan of a family-owned business is only twenty-four years. In fact, according to businessweek.com, only about 40 percent of US family-owned businesses transition to the second generation, while approximately 13 percent are passed down successfully to a third generation, and a measly 3 percent survive to a fourth generation or beyond. Some of this is due to changing markets or poor decisions in leadership, but much of it is due to family dynamics turning toxic and bleeding into the business.

And unfortunately, these statistics speak to issues that relate to family businesses of every size and shape. Back when I worked in the IT department for a family business, I was once in a room with Max Hopper, a senior vice president at American Airlines at the time. He said something to me that I've found to remain true. In discussing the various difficulties his company was facing compared to his competitors, he said, "We're all facing the same issues; it's just the number of zeros after the number that's different."

That's the case with family businesses. The Roy family of *Succession* is dealing with the same issues as millions of family businesses; there are just more zeroes after the number for them. Their difficulties are, in many ways, the same difficulties that Peter was dealing with. The same jealousies and ambitions we see on television are playing out in businesses across the country.

This dysfunction can take on many forms. Sometimes, it's high drama perfect for a TV show or a biblical parable. Sometimes, it looks almost pedestrian. Consider this scenario. You hire your sister-in-law's son to stack crates, but he assumes he doesn't have to show up on time or do the work to get a paycheck. The rest of your staff resents him, but if you fire him, you'll have to deal with your sister-in-law's anger at the family's annual Thanksgiving dinner.

What do you do?

What would you do if you were Peter and your middle son was likely to struggle without your help—but if you help, you alienate your other children? Many of us would, out of perceived familial obligations, make business decisions that are not in the best interests of the business or the child.

"What would you do?" That's often the hardest question to answer. Some family tension and some business issues are inevitable, but founders often struggle to identify what kind of solution would work when family problems and business problems become deeply entangled.

Too often, they choose a family solution to a business problem or a business solution to a family problem. Or they simply do nothing because they don't see any good options.

It's time to change that. There are better tools available to tackle the family business troubles you're facing—tools that can offer a way forward that doesn't look like the Roy family.

THE BEST OF BOTH WORLDS

With the right organization and frameworks in place, you can separate family and business issues so that both can thrive without drama. Through these changes, you can create guardrails that avoid some of the most common ways that family naturally runs into trouble in business. For instance, it's natural for siblings to have a certain amount of rivalry, and it's natural that parents want to give their children everything. These natural instincts, though, can lead to trouble in a business.

To avoid that trouble, you have to put the right structures in place, so you can separate those family dynamics from your business decisions.

I've lived this process myself. My daughter, Staci, runs our family printing business. As her father, it would be easy for me to let her off the hook for everything. When my wife and I were younger, we had tough times. There was a period when we lived in an apartment, and we had to hope the check arrived on time so we could afford to eat. I don't want Staci to ever have to live that kind of struggle. I want to give her the world. But I also don't want her to take anything for granted.

In the same way I was willing to buy her a car at sixteen but made her get a job to pay for gas, I've endeavored to create frameworks so that she has learned the value of work and understands accountability while also succeeding in her position and learning to be a leader.

This book is about putting those systems in place throughout your business. With these ideas, you can enjoy the benefits of family business—the trust, the love, the security—while limiting the risk of those negative issues.

FAMILY AND BUSINESS ARE NOT EASY

You could say I've been doing the research for this book my entire life. I've been a part of family businesses from my childhood right up to the present day. I grew up working with my father at his service station. Early in my career, I worked on the tech side of a billion-dollar family business. I've started multiple family businesses since, and now, as I've already mentioned, I own the business my daughter runs. Most significantly, though, I've spent twenty-three years as a certified business coach focused primarily on helping family businesses thrive.

I've learned a lot about what processes and frameworks need to be in place for family business to run smoothly. Through it all, I've managed to build a loving family and several successful businesses without falling into the kinds of difficulties that plague so many family businesses today. Now, it's time to share all that I've learned.

The first lesson I want to share is that this stuff is difficult. Anyone who's ever been the founder of a family or a business knows that success isn't easy. So, it should not be surprising that the ideas in this book, while sometimes simple to understand, are rarely easy to fully implement. It will take time and commitment to get where you want to be. But every founder also knows that nothing is more important than getting family and business right.

Additionally, I want to state here that some of the work ahead may fall outside the scope of this book. It takes wisdom to know which problems require a business solution and which ones require a family solution. Ahead, we'll cover the business solutions. The family solutions are for another book.

For instance, we'll look at how you can keep siblings apart who don't get along. We'll look at how you can limit the ways the business might inflame their rivalry. We'll discuss how to find each sibling a role that's right for them. But we won't discuss how you repair their relationship. Put another way, I'm a business coach. For some issues, you may need a family counselor.

That said, it's no exaggeration to say that this book may hold the key to saving your family and your business. The risks of ignoring family or business could not be higher. I've seen families ripped apart. I've seen companies go bankrupt. And sometimes, you run out of time to rebuild what's been broken.

A friend of mine, Kevin N. Lawrence, wrote a book a few years ago called *Your Oxygen Mask First*. During the rollout for the book, he led a group of coaches I was a part of. There, he described a billionaire who had everything—except peace. His business was thriving. He had all the money in the world. In the end, though, he took his own life.

You can have peace at home and prosperity in the office, but you're going to have to work for them—and you need to start immediately. At least now you'll have a manifesto that shows what you need to do to make family business work.

PART I

WHY FAMILY BUSINESS?

CHAPTER 1

THE VALUE OF FAMILY BUSINESS

MUCH OF THE BOOK AHEAD WILL FOCUS ON ALL THE WAYS family business can go wrong and how you avoid that happening. For that reason, I want to start with an insight that may seem so obvious we can almost forget it: family business is really great.

Think about the most successful companies in the world. On any given list, it's likely that several of them are family businesses. BMW and Ford Motor Company are family businesses. So are Comcast and Carnival Corporation. Chick-fil-A is the largest chicken sandwich company in the world and is famously still entirely owned by the Cathy family.

Walmart is the planet's largest private employer and one of its largest companies. The Walton family still owns just under half of it.

In other words, there really is no limit to the potential of family business—when it's run right.

THE ENGINE OF THE ECONOMY

Family businesses aren't just at the top of the Fortune 500 list; they are huge drivers of our entire economy. It's no exaggeration to say that family business is one of the greatest assets of the American economy.

According to *Fortune*, 87 percent of businesses in America are family owned. They make up 54 percent of our GDP and employ 59 percent of people. While large, faceless corporations tend to make most of the headlines, it's the family businesses that hold our economy together.

And this is really only scratching the surface. In a study by Jess H. Chua, James J. Chrisman, and Erick P. C. Chang titled *Are Family Firms Born or Made?*, they found that most businesses wouldn't even get off the ground without family. According to the study, 77 percent of all new business ventures involve some form of family involvement from the very start. A further 3 percent of companies see family involvement start within the first two years.

Without family business, then, we'd lack many of our business leaders. We'd see half our companies disappear, and we'd hardly have an entrepreneurial economy at all.

OPPORTUNITIES FOR ALL

There's a reason so many businesses bring family in. While it's nice to be a driver of the US economy, that's not why most of us get into family business. Instead, we do it because we believe we can rely on family. We start family businesses primarily because we believe that we can trust the members of our family above all others. If anyone is going to work hard and give us honest feedback, it'll be family.

At the same time, if the business succeeds, it'll help the people we care about most in many ways. It's a win–win for everyone who matters to us, sometimes in ways we don't even realize.

GENERATIONAL WEALTH AND SECURITY

This is one of the strongest dreams of the family business founder. We want to create the opportunity to build wealth for our families today and in the future after we're gone. And this is a reasonable dream with family business. If done correctly, you can change the family tree for generations.

Many founders have already seen this benefit in their lives. According to an OnStartups article in 2009, 48.1 percent of entrepreneurs grew up in a family business. They saw their own parents, aunts and uncles, or grandparents build success and share it. It's only natural to want to continue that tradition on their own.

And when starting a business, it just makes sense to organize it in a way that will most benefit the people we care about most. Why give your wealth to outsiders who don't value you, your family, or the company? Why not allow family to grow as the business grows and give the opportunities business creates to family?

Every parent knows that keen desire to provide a good life to their children. For many, family business makes that desire a reality.

PASSING ON YOUR JOY

We all dream of passing on something beyond monetary security to our children. We want to share our values, provide them with the tools to create happiness in their lives, and give them a piece of ourselves to remember us by. A family business offers the opportunity to do all three at once. Instead of simply retiring when you finish work, wouldn't it be so much better to pass on your life's work to those who care as much as you do?

The current CEO of a local landscape supply company is the second generation of the family to run the company. He's currently in the process of grooming the next generation to take over. When I recently spoke to Steve Mann, the current CEO, he said of his son, "He's doing stuff I couldn't even imagine doing."

That's the dream, isn't it? We all want to pass along our company to family members who will care as much as we do and who will bring their own unique skills and ideas to the business.

And along the way, we want to pass along the values that allowed us to succeed in the first place. We want to be like the Walton family who still uphold Walmart founder Sam Walton's values in how they run the company. And whether you agree with them or not, the Cathy family behind Chick-fil-A still uphold founder S. Truett Cathy's beliefs and values.

We'd all like to see our family businesses become part of that tradition.

CREATING A CAREER PATH FOR WOMEN

For many of us, there's particular value in family business in offering opportunities to those in our family who have to face an uneven playing field. In particular, many of us believe that family business can create the space for the women in our families to show just how talented and capable they are.

According to a 2007 article in *Fortune* magazine, there are far more women in top positions in family businesses than in the wider business world. At that time, 24 percent of family businesses had a female CEO or president. Even better, 31.3 percent had a woman next in line to take over the company. And according to a 2008 MassMutual American Family Business Survey, the percentage of family businesses with women in the highest levels of management was close to sixty.

Some of those numbers may still seem low when women make up almost half the workforce but compare them to the leadership of Fortune 500 companies, where the number of women in top leadership positions was only 13.8 percent in 2015.

The numbers on this are very clear. If you care about the women in your family having the chance to show all they can do, it's far better for them to do so within a family business.

STRENGTHENING COMMUNITY

Beyond family concerns, most family business founders would like to be a positive influence on their communities. We all know that those large corporations that overrun communities aren't interested in doing what's best for our town or our state. A family business can be an engine for good values and strong ethics that can help strengthen the places we care about most.

This is the consensus among family business founders. According to that same Mass Mutual American Family Business Survey I referenced above, almost 60 percent of founders thought they held their company to a higher ethical standard than other companies. More than a third had discussed their ethics with employees and others in their community, not just once but regularly.

A Family Enterprise USA 2013 Survey of Family Firms found that, "Successful family firms embrace a sense of stewardship and fiscal responsibility, and they expect our government to do the same."

Family businesses, in other words, instill strong, positive values that can have a ground-up benefit for our towns, cities, states, and country.

A BLESSING AND A CURSE

These are all very good reasons to start and grow a family business. We work with the people we care about, share the wealth across our families, create opportunities where our spouses, siblings, and children can thrive, and improve our communities. When done right, family business also clearly allows for companies to succeed at the highest level. I personally believe in all these benefits.

But for all the positive potential, there is so much that can go wrong when you bring family and business together. A 2012 PricewaterhouseCoopers Family Business survey found that almost a third of all founders were uncertain about transferring their business to the next generation. And with good reason, as we've already seen, only 40 percent of family businesses make it through the second generation of leadership.

And the risks of family business can happen to anyone. I once worked with a billion-dollar company run by two brothers. One of them was the founder and CEO, the other was the CFO. For years, everything was going along well. The brothers were close, and they kept family drama out of the office—until one day, when they got into a vicious argument. Locked in the CEO's office, on a floor with 150 of their employees, these two men in their fifties started screaming at each other.

The argument ended with the CFO shouting, "Mom always liked you better," before slamming the door and walking out of the office.

These kinds of issues can come up any time there is a misalignment between family and business practices. And it doesn't require anyone behaving poorly for everything to go wrong.

Another client of mine ran an HVAC company. Kevin, the founder, and his wife, Lisa, had been in charge of the company for twenty-five years. They had built it into a two-million-dollar-a-year business. They wanted to retire, and they were preparing for their son, Bryan, to take over.

There was just one problem: Bryan didn't have the interest or talents for that role. Instead, he'd gone to school to become a high school baseball coach. He loved his job, and he was great at it.

However, because he was also a dutiful son, when his parents asked him to leave his job and take over the HVAC company, he agreed. This is what Kevin had always wanted for his son, and Bryan didn't want to disappoint anyone. After all, Bryan convinced himself, there were lots of benefits beyond pleasing Mom and Dad. Running the HVAC company would represent a big boost in his income. He could get up later and be home more often with his young family.

Everyone was doing exactly what they were supposed to do, thinking about family and trying to take care of everyone. But it all ended up in disaster. Bryan had no idea how to run an HVAC company or how to be a manager of an experienced team who were almost all older than him. He came in trying to run the company the way he coached a high school team. As a coach, he had a "what I say goes" attitude the kids responded well to. His new team did not respond well.

At the same time, in an effort to make the business his own, he started introducing radical changes without understanding the consequences. That "what I say goes" attitude meant there was no room for feedback.

Trying to stave off disaster, Kevin called me in to arbitrate for everyone. Bryan realized his mistakes, apologized to the team, and started going on jobs to learn more about the trade. Kevin agreed to stay in the company a little longer and slow down the transition.

It might have all turned out okay in the end, but the family had less time to correct their mistakes than they thought. After another long day at the office, Kevin came home one evening, sat down in his favorite chair, and died. Without him there to hold Bryan's hand as he got up to speed, the company unraveled quickly.

Lisa and Bryan closed everything down within a year, leaving Bryan searching for another high school coaching job.

I know, hearing stories like that, the natural instinct is to say that can't happen to you. In fact, facing those risks, maybe you want to say that you don't even run a family business. You just have a business with family connected to it. But the truth is, no matter how family connects to business, if it connects all, there's real risk ahead if you don't watch out.

CHAPTER 2

A FAMILY BUSINESS... WHETHER YOU LIKE IT OR NOT

A NUMBER OF YEARS BACK NOW, I WAS COACHING A LANDscaping company that was owned by a married couple. The company developed almost by accident. Dave was the landscaper. After a number of years working for other people, he decided he wanted to start his own business. Once he did, success came faster than he was expecting. He was a hard worker who really took care of his customers. Because of that, his business grew almost without effort. When he started landing some commercial clients, his wife, Janice, suggested they borrow some money from her mother and expand.

With that loan, they were able to buy trucks and equipment and hire a crew. From there, things just kept growing. Janice became the office manager, handling accounts, scheduling, and the team. Dave moved into sales and managing the crews while on the job.

Before they knew it, they had a three-million-dollar business. Surveying their success, they decided they wanted to really scale dramatically. So they came to me.

They were both eager, but after a few meetings, we still couldn't make any progress. Each time they came in, they seemed to get into arguments over next steps. Because they couldn't come to an agreement on anything, we couldn't plan out their strategy.

After this had happened a few times, I got out the org chart. "Let's step back a moment," I said, "and talk about company organization. Who is the head of your company?"

Incredibly, they both said at the very same time, "I am."

I glanced at both of them. "Okay," I said, "I'm just curious here—if you don't agree, who has the final say?"

Once again, both of them simultaneously said, "I do."

That threw gas on the fire. What followed was the biggest argument I've ever witnessed. They got so loud, my colleagues on the other side of our enormous office had to stop working.

Dave insisted that this was ultimately his company because it was built off his work. But Janice countered that it was her mother who offered the initial loan.

"You wouldn't have a company without my family!" she shouted.

"Without me, you couldn't do anything with your mom's money!" Dave shouted back.

After about fifteen minutes of this, I stepped in.

"You don't need me," I said. "You need a marriage counselor."

They left in a huff. We had a few more meetings after that, but within four months, they had filed for divorce. They ended up dissolving the company along the way.

SO MANY WAYS TO ORGANIZE A BUSINESS

Before that argument, I don't think Dave and Janice ever really thought of their company as a family business. It was just their business, and they happened to be family. Unlike some founders, they hadn't consciously jumped into family business for the reasons I covered in the last chapter. It had just been more convenient to get the loan from Janice's mom than going to a bank. It had just been easier to bring Janice in for office management than to hire someone. And since the company was both of their idea, they both ran it.

It may never have crossed their minds at all that they had to attend to the extra risks of bringing family and business together. But that was definitely the case.

For that reason, I want to take a moment here to describe just how broad the category of family business is. Because whether you like it or not, if your company falls into any of the descriptions below, you need all the advice ahead to avoid the risks that come with family business.

Let's start with a definition. Essentially, I define a family business as *any company in which family plays even a small part.* There's a lot of intentional vagueness in that definition precisely because family business can take on so many forms. In reality, all businesses are family businesses, they include family, or support the families of the team members.

The most common type of family business is one with direct family involvement. This includes all the most obvious ways family comes into business. The most common family business organization is the one Dave and Janice unconsciously fell into. In this setup, a founder and their spouse build the business together. One of them usually manages the business, and the other handles the back-office work, such as accounting, HR, and so on.

We'll see this setup throughout the book. And while we'll touch on this in more depth just below, it's worth stating here that this organization is not always formal. Peter, whom we met in the Introduction, ran his plumbing and franchise hardware store business. His wife, Susan, didn't have a technical role in the company. But she had always consulted on important decisions and helped out on the back end when Peter was overwhelmed or was short-staffed in the office.

The next most common family business organization is parents and their children. Once again, Peter's company falls into this category, as well as many of the family businesses I mentioned in the last chapter. Ultimately, many of us consciously create a *family* business precisely so our children can someday enter it. This is a noble aim, but there's a darker side to this ambition, one that includes the parents' desire to maintain influence well into the adulthood of their children, using family business as the vehicle.

After children, there are many family businesses run by siblings. And beyond that, there are all kinds of configurations in which family members play a direct role. You can have cousins, uncles and aunts, and in-laws of all kinds with positions within the company. You might have a business in which your niece handles sales or your second cousin's stepbrother manages the shop floor.

If family of any sort is working within the company, it's a family business. And this can also include those who are *like* family. I've worked with a CEO who ran a company in which his father's best friend's children worked under him. Those kids, though, were essentially family. The two families had been so close, the same rules applied.

ANY RELATIONSHIP TO BUSINESS COUNTS

Sometimes, family's connection to the business is very straightforward—you employ your children or you and your sister co-own a company—but that isn't always the case. Family can enter a business in a million different ways. And sometimes, the route is so circuitous, you don't notice the change.

Take Dave and Janice. Janice's mother may have made that loan without ever explicitly saying she wanted any influence in the business. She may never have injected herself into business matters. Yet, as soon as that argument over control began, Janice used that loan as leverage to prove she should call the shots.

This had nothing to do with her mother's wishes. Sometimes, parents do act only as investors and are not active in the business. I call this "the bank of Dad." But that still counts as family business.

And it could just as easily have gone a different way. Her mother could have come in five years after the loan was paid back and suggested she should have some say in how things are run. Or she could ask that Dave and Janice employ one of her grandchildren as thanks for the favor she did for them with the loan. Whenever you take someone's money—even a parent's—there is an assumption that they will have some level of control and power.

This doesn't have to involve money, either. If you consult with your father about your business when you start out, he may feel he is entitled to know the inner workings from then on. He may feel he should at least be heard out every time you make a big decision from then on.

You may create a partnership between your restaurant and your cousin's butcher shop to provide all the meat each week. That also creates family business dynamics.

Your sister may do a few shifts for your company when you start out while she's home from college. But she may feel that entitles her to a position for her daughter in the company twenty years later when the daughter is the one in college.

The truth is, anytime family is introduced to the business in any capacity, it becomes a family business. As soon as you offer a family member a job, as soon as you take a loan, ask for advice, or ask for a favor, your business is exposed to the same risks all family businesses face.

In fact, your business may face these risks without ever including any family in it. Simply having a successful business can lead family to seek a way into it. A family member could ask for loans because they know you're doing well. They could ask for a job because they know your company is growing. They could seek references, huge discounts on your products or services, or any number of inside benefits. And simply wanting those things can build pressure across the family, pushing for you to create a family business accommodation.

In other words, no matter how tangential family is to your business, the risks are there. And that means you have to be prepared for them.

ALL FAMILY BUSINESSES ARE AT RISK

Dale, a client of mine, came to me recently with a dilemma. Six months earlier, his cousin had asked him to hire her son for a job at his family trucking business. It was an entry-level position stacking pallets, but the kid took the job for granted. He'd show up late and refuse to do his part. After a few weeks of this, my client did the natural thing any employer would do: Dale fired him.

But when it comes to family business, things are never that straightforward. That decision rippled throughout his family. He got an angry call from his cousin who had, of course, only heard the story through her son, who bewailed how mean old Uncle Dale had mistreated him. His cousin's son started gossiping about Dale's daughter and her husband, saying they were going to get divorced because he'd seen them arguing once. This was an exaggeration bordering on a lie, but that didn't matter. The damage had been done.

Worst of all, this behavior drove a wedge between Dale's cousin's son and his daughter, who had previously been almost like siblings. The whole family was at odds, and Dale had no clue how to repair the damage.

Not every family business situation is as dramatic as that, and they certainly aren't always as dramatic as what happened to Dave and Janice. But bringing family and business together can create a million problems small and large that can endanger prosperity in the office and peace in the home.

It can lead to a cycle of conflict in the office that leads to conflict at home. Or the conflict at home can lead to conflict in the office. If you want to protect yourself from these cycles, we need to understand why things break down between family and business. Only then can we see how we can fix it.

CHAPTER 3

WHY FAMILY BUSINESSES FAIL

WE ALL KNOW THE STORY OF CAIN AND ABEL, BUT TOO often, it's easy to see it as a well-worn metaphor or a piece of ancient history. In truth, the patterns of behavior we see in that story still describe how family relationships can fail.

I once advised a family business in the midst of its succession process after the founder suddenly died. Beth, his wife, had been left in charge. She, in turn, decided to hand the company over to one of her children. She had two sons: Alexander, the elder, and Cameron, the younger. She also had a daughter, Claire.

Alexander was the success of the family. Strong, intelligent, and charming, he'd played college football before climbing his way to the top of the business world. Cameron, on the other hand, had been the dutiful one. He was smaller and had fewer innate gifts, but he had been the one to stick around and help his father build the company.

Since Claire showed no interest in leadership, Beth had to choose between her two sons. Instead of weighing the options carefully, she made a fateful, shortsighted decision. Alexander was older, so Beth decided he should become CEO. Cameron would remain in his position as VP of sales. Upon getting the news, Alexander quit his job as an executive at a company in a completely different industry and took over.

Almost immediately, Beth's decision led to serious problems in the family and the business. It started with Claire. She had also entered the business young, but unlike Cameron, she'd never put much effort into the work. She'd felt entitled to a good paycheck, and her father had allowed her to shuffle along without much pushback. Alexander decided he wanted to run things differently. When Claire consistently failed to deliver on projects, he fired her.

That decision blew up in his face. After she was fired, Claire cut off all communication with the family. The pain of the situation nearly killed Beth.

That would have been more than enough for any family business to take, but there were also issues with Cameron. Alexander was pushing for him to expand sales, but Cameron was proving unwilling. He was in charge of the main account for the business, which brought in 90 percent of their revenue. When asked to do more, he would agree to Alexander's face but then never follow through.

In frustration, Alexander called me in.

After hearing him out, I said, "To know how you should respond, you have to decide what you do *not* want to do to get where you want to go. So what are you *not* willing to do to improve sales?"

Alexander was unequivocal: "I don't want to fire my brother. Firing Claire nearly destroyed the family. I won't put Mom through that again."

"Well then," I said, "you've got to resolve whatever issues

there are with your brother. I can't help you until you find a way to talk it out and find a solution together."

It took months for the two of them to get into a room and lay out their problems.

Once they were together, Cameron finally revealed the Cain-like jealousy at the heart of his behavior: "I don't think you should be CEO. I was the one who worked my way up in the business. I was the one who stuck around. You got all the glory, and now Mom has handed you another success on a plate. But guess what? I don't respect you, and I won't help you succeed."

Alexander was flummoxed. All he could respond was, "What did I do?"

But it didn't matter that Alexander had never consciously harmed Cameron. Cameron had spent his life building up resentments against him. Alexander was older, taller, stronger, smarter, more handsome, more charismatic, and more successful. Cameron couldn't take it that his mother had also given Alexander the job Cameron had worked so hard for.

Once the truth was out, there was too much toxicity to salvage anything. Within a couple months, Cameron had quit, taking the company's main client with him to his new business. The family business folded shortly afterward.

AN AWKWARD ARRANGEMENT

It's hard to feel either Alexander or Cameron was completely wrong. Alexander had done no one any harm and didn't even know Cameron was resentful. But Cameron also had reason to feel he'd been passed over when Beth chose his brother.

This is the real, underlying issue with all family businesses. It brings together two complicated types of relationship and removes the obvious solutions to problems in either.

In a normal business, if someone behaved like Cameron, you'd replace him. But Alexander didn't feel he could fire Cameron. That family relationship made it impossible, as he'd discovered with Claire. To fire Cameron could harm the family, so Cameron had to stay.

At the same time, in a normal family, if you don't get along with someone, you can usually avoid them. This is what Cameron had done with Alexander for years before their father died. Cameron had only had to see Alexander at holidays, where it wasn't too hard to be nice for a day or so at a time.

But once they were in business together, it was impossible to avoid one another. They had to work together, and Cameron was forced to work for the person he resented most.

These issues are further complicated by the fact that family business necessarily draws together people with long, shared histories. Unlike a normal business relationship that can start fresh or can be kept professional, family relationships have decades of old wounds that come with them. Cameron was still upset that Alexander had been a successful football player in high school and college. He could still remember every time he had felt like Alexander had picked on him as a child.

There's no starting over with those relationships when you're in a business together. Those old feelings naturally creep in. And if they were hard to resolve around the dinner table, they're even harder to handle in the boardroom.

Those old, broken relationships can then cause all kinds of knock-on problems. Instead of family members trying to help one another succeed, sometimes, as with Cameron, they want one another to fail.

Other times, it simply becomes impossible to trust one another. Stephen R. Covey wrote a book called *The Speed of Trust* in which he pointed out that you can't demand trust, you have to build it through relationships. Trust is earned. But those same family relationships that are meant to build trust can destroy it. They can destroy it in an instant—when a spouse cheats or a child drunkenly drives the family car into a ditch—or it can be lost a little bit at a time. If your sibling always promises to be on time but always arrives late, each time you trust them a little less.

One of the pitfalls of this dynamic is that we naturally ascribe motives to behaviors. We tend to do this more with family than with those who aren't. And when trust is lost, we assume the worst. We assume family are showing up late because they are trying to get back at us or because they still hold a grudge. It may or may not be true, but we do it all the same.

And this is just the beginning. Broken trust can leave room for all sorts of issues to develop in the family business.

COMMON FAMILY BUSINESS ISSUES

We all know that families face all kinds of complicated dynamics. Often, these are relatively natural and innocent problems that we all work through. There are little jealousies, miscommunications, and misaligned feelings of entitlement. When there is love and trust in the family, we work through these things.

But when those feelings are damaged, and when we lack structure to keep things from getting worse, any number of problems can develop that can prove fatal to family and business.

CONSTANT COMPARISON

Even if you've never watched *The Brady Bunch*, you've probably heard the line, "Marcia, Marcia, Marcia!" It was spoken by Marcia's little sister, Jan, who felt her older sister got all the praise and attention.

The line has stuck with us because it describes a very common feeling, particularly among siblings. It often feels like our brothers or sisters get all the love and affection.

It's basic human nature to compare ourselves to others, and particularly to those we are closest to. In and of itself, this urge to compare is healthy. It can even be positive, allowing us to see our best qualities more clearly or give us a sense of where we could improve.

But when it goes wrong in families, it can create room for resentment. And resentment in business can destroy everything. Because Cameron had felt that his family had always been about "Alexander, Alexander, Alexander!," he couldn't swallow his resentment and work for his older brother. The comparison ruined any chance that everyone could work together toward the same goals.

ASSUMING THE WORST

In the absence of enough information, we tend to jump to conclusions—and unless we truly trust those responsible for the decision at hand, we usually assume the worst. This is innate to how our brains work. We have what psychologists call a negativity bias in which we overemphasize the negative aspects of every situation.

This helps us survive. After all, if you were out in the woods, it would be far better to assume the worst when you hear rustling in the distance than to assume the best and end up getting eaten by some wild animal.

But in practice, in family business, it means that we often ascribe negative motives to every decision if it isn't fully explained. Did Dad give your sister the COO role because he loves and trusts her more? Did Mom call you out on the shop floor because she thinks you're unworthy of the job she gave you?

Cameron assumed the worst of his mother's decision to give Alexander the top job at their company. Because she didn't explain her reasoning very well, he filled in all the gaps with the negative feelings he had built up over a lifetime.

Assumption works both ways. Parents sometimes ascribe negative qualities to their children for certain behaviors. When my daughter, Staci, started school, we kept hearing that she had a discipline issue. After about the fourth call, I told the administrator that Staci didn't have an issue. She behaved very well for us at home, and we had always been very good about discipline.

Eventually, we realized that she had ADHD and needed medication. But the assumption of some of the adults in her life was that this was a personal fault of hers.

We can see these assumptions very clearly with issues of mental health or addiction. Often, parents will assume that these issues are due to some fault in their child or some fault in their parenting. Such assumptions don't always have to come from such dramatic situations either. Many parents read their child's poor behavior at work as a reflection of their parenting, and their sense of guilt motivates them to keep their children in the job.

This is precisely what happened with Alexander's sister, Claire. Their father felt he must have failed her in some way, reading a rebuke of his parenting in her refusal to work. And so he kept protecting her, kept giving her money, and kept moving her up the business—even though that wasn't really helping anyone.

SEEKING VALIDATION

While family members are often assuming the worst, they're also always seeking validation from one another. Since every decision seems to have a deeper meaning, and since we're always in competition with one another, family members will end up competing for validation through their work in the business.

It's easy, then, to see how much Beth's decision to give Alexander the top role must have stung Cameron. After years of trying to earn validation by working hard in the business, he was passed over for his more successful brother.

Feeling spurned by his family, he became set on destroying everything.

ENTITLEMENT

Not all children are obsessed with getting validation from their parents. Unfortunately, many of them feel entitled not only to validation but to enjoying the fruits of their parents' success without putting the work in themselves.

This was clearly how Claire felt with her own family's business. She felt that success was owed to her. She didn't feel she needed to work hard or provide value in order to deserve a sizable paycheck.

It's a hard truth for founders to swallow, but it's true nonetheless: some children are mature enough to understand the opportunity and responsibility that comes with family business from the beginning. But many—perhaps even most—are not.

Sometimes, this is a phase. While I was generally a good worker for my father. I have to admit that there were times when I felt I could slack off. After all, what was the boss going to do to me? Yell at me? He already did that at home. And he needed me at the service station. If I didn't get things done on time, he'd just have to wait.

Again, that was only for a brief period. I grew out of it. But many children continue to feel that way throughout life. And to be honest, it's usually partly the founder's fault.

Founders often hold back corrective action against their children—in the business and sometimes even at home. Whether out of guilt, a fear of confrontation, or a misplaced desire to nurture, they tolerate bad behavior. And as legendary football coach Tom Landry once put it: "You get what you demand; you encourage what you tolerate."

TOP-DOWN AUTHORITY

Entitlement doesn't all go one way. In other words, it isn't just the kids who can feel entitled to something. Unfortunately, I also experienced this in my father's business. He had a certain "you owe me" attitude. He'd worked hard to build his service station, and he expected me to be grateful for that—which I was. But he expected me to be so grateful that I'd give up on all my own dreams and take over when he was ready to retire.

He never asked me if I wanted to do that. He never even communicated that's what he expected. It was only when I got a scholarship and decided to go to college that it became clear just how much his plans rested on that unspoken expectation.

I wish I could say otherwise, but the fact is my father never truly forgave me for living my own life. He kicked me out the day I left for college, and I never moved back in again. Our relationship never fully recovered.

This can sometimes be the way with founders. They want a top-down structure, almost like the military. They introduce a "don't question what I say, just do what I say" attitude. But children will naturally resist their parents. They will naturally develop their own ideas and ambitions. And if founders aren't careful, they can lose not just a business partner but their relationship with their children.

A good business has leadership that can inspire everyone to

go in the same direction. But it also allows feedback to ensure the best decision always gets made. When it comes to family business, though, parental authority can get in the way of that.

A founder has to own their authority in the home and the office to reduce entitlement in their children, but if they aren't flexible enough, they can chase away the people they care about most.

BEING ADULTS

Relatedly, it can be incredibly difficult to pull ourselves out of old parent–child dynamics when we enter the office. How many times, when your child was growing up, did you run into this scenario? You told them to do something, and they responded with, "Why do I need to do this?" To which you answered, "Because I said so."

Just because your kids have grown up and you're meeting them in a professional setting doesn't mean that dynamic has shifted. In fact, it's often deeply entrenched, even if the words you use now are slightly different.

The psychiatrist Eric Berne broke down these dynamics into several different categories in what is called "transactional analysis theory." In interactions, we fall into one of several categories:

- The Natural Child: This is the creative, playful, spontaneous version of ourselves—the version who could build things with LEGO pieces for hours and create whole worlds in our minds.
- The Adapted Child: This is the version of ourselves that conforms but also rebels. We do what we're told, but we also have within us that ability to push back.

- The Critical Parent: This is our judgmental parental side, telling others what they can and can't do and always finding something to criticize.
- The Nurturing Parent: This is our maternal side, the one that excuses everything, wants to do everything to help others, and offers unconditional care.

These dynamics are at play when we try to work with family. Often, we fall into one of these categories while the other person plays another part. We're overly critical and demanding, while the other person is accommodating but potentially rebellious. We're nurturing while they are creative and free spirited.

The problem is that you can't get much business done when people are trapped in these dynamics. Instead, you need everyone to be in a final state: the adult state. This is where we can function logically and act in the present.

Most of us are in the adult state regularly. But it's much harder to enter it with family who bring those other dynamics into our interactions.

BUILD A STRUCTURE TO REDUCE THESE TENSIONS

By the time I was brought in to coach Alexander's company, it was too late to save it. But it isn't too late for you.

Every one of the issues we've covered in this chapter involve choices that family members are making in the family business. The key word there is "choice." In other words, we have some control over this.

Facing the struggles of family, business, and family business head on is a great first step to creating space for solutions. Simply by reading this first part of the book, you've done that.

But once you create that space, there's so much we can do

to reduce the risk that your company will follow the path that Alexander's did. Emotional intelligence, for instance, is one of the most critical leadership skills, yet it seems to go away when we're dealing with family. We have to change that, creating space for us to meet one another as adults and treat one another well within the business.

In particular, there are two kinds of changes you can make in your company to create that dynamic. First, you can strengthen the business fundamentals so the business runs more smoothly and successfully. These business basics allow you to improve how the company operates as a company. You can get better with your finances and strategy, for instance. You can create a stronger understanding of the roles you need to fill in the company and who best fills them. The better you run the company, the less likely family issues will come up.

But that won't be enough to protect your family and your business. For that, you need to make a second set of changes and add some family-focused solutions to your business. These frameworks and mindsets can clarify your priorities, improve communication, and create the structures that allow everyone to grow into their role and know where they belong.

When you combine these solutions, you can minimize the opportunity for all those family problems to explode in the business. And you can finally get some peace at home and prosperity in the office.

PART II

BUSINESS BASICS

CHAPTER 4

KNOW YOUR NUMBERS

WE MET PETER AND HIS FAMILY IN THE INTRODUCTION. Peter's four children all worked in his business, and there were issues with each. His oldest, Eric, was trying to take control of the company while Peter was still in charge. Zach, his second son, refused to do the work but felt entitled to a big paycheck. And the youngest of the family, Sam, didn't want anything to do with any of it. He just wanted to run his part of the business and be left alone.

It was a real mess, and that mess started not with any of Peter's sons but with his daughter, Jessica.

Jessica was the first child to enter the family business. While Eric was away at school and Zach and Sam were too young to take a position, Jessica ran the family's plumbing company with her husband, Rich. They were competent managers, and at first, it looked like this was a perfect fit. The plumbing company was growing at a decent if unremarkable pace.

But Peter started to notice that Jessica and Rich were spending less and less time in the office. It turned out, they were taking their bonus money and investing in rental properties. They were buying distressed multifamily housing and restoring them, partly with the help of the plumbing company. When Peter asked them about it, they confessed that their true long-term goal was to build their own rental property empire.

If this were any normal corporation, it would be an admirable strategy. But this was a family business that Peter had dedicated everything to. It was a company he'd brought them into at the top level—with the expectation that they'd use that privileged position to help him continue to grow the business. Instead of showing gratitude and dedicating themselves to helping the family business run well, they were using it to build a separate company right under Peter's nose.

To make matters worse, they'd clearly known this would upset Peter and kept it from him as long as possible.

When Peter did predictably get upset, they threw their own grievances back at him. Peter had promised to create a system to give them increasing equity in the plumbing company the longer they stayed. Peter still meant to do that, but he had to admit he hadn't gotten around to it yet—and Jessica and Rich had noticed. Now, they wanted more than just the equity in the company they were owed; they also wanted equity in some of Peter's other companies.

Peter's a fair guy. He came back and offered them a small percentage of equity in the plumbing company *and* his stores. But he also insisted they pay for some of the costs for the company and stores. "You can't have all the profits and none of the expenses," he pointed out. "If you want in on this, you have to absorb some of the risk."

He anticipated that they might want to negotiate on the deal. He was willing to give a little on the expenses or to adjust slightly on the equity. Instead, they walked away from the company completely. They also heavily reduced their communication with Peter and his wife, Susan.

By that time, Sam was old enough to join the business and was looking for a good opportunity. Unlike Jessica, he was very interested in actually running the plumbing company. When Peter put him in charge, Sam poured everything into it. He turned out to be a good leader. He worked well with the team and built up the business faster than anyone expected.

Peter was impressed. Where Jessica and Rich had been competent in leadership, Sam really flourished.

But he had his own complaints. Along with having to deal with his brothers always fighting, he also bristled at a practice Peter had instituted across all his companies. He would take from those doing very well to fund those he was growing. In practice, this meant he took from Sam's profits in the plumbing company to pay for franchise stores he'd recently bought that weren't yet cash positive.

These were retail stores, which require a lot of inventory. This was a new area of business for Peter, and he couldn't quite make the numbers work. Each month, some stores had too much inventory; some had too little. The numbers seemed to change every month. This required extra investment to overstock until things evened out. And Sam's success in plumbing was paying for this strategy.

Again, in any other kind of business, this would be a reasonable policy. Corporations take from profitable departments to scale up other areas all the time. And Peter was entitled to do what he wanted with his companies. But that wasn't an excuse Sam would accept.

At one point, Sam stormed into his father's office. "I'm always strapped for cash even though I'm running things profitably," he shouted. "Why do I have to pay for your bad business decisions? I don't want to go into debt just because you can't balance your books."

They were harsh words, but Peter had to admit, Sam did have a point. While this strategy was completely justifiable, Peter realized he hadn't been as clear in his financial situation as he could have been—with Sam or with Jessica. He could have drawn up plans for equity sooner. He could have been more transparent about his business costs. He could have made the inventory issue a priority.

As he mulled all this over, he saw that the only way to solve these family business problems was for him to get a better hold of the numbers driving his companies.

FOLLOW THE MONEY

Peter's family business problems were complicated, as we'll see throughout the book. Even if he had his finances in perfect order, he would have lacked the peace at home and prosperity in the office he was craving. But increasing his understanding of his company's finances would have undeniably helped relieve some of the stressors in his relationship with Jessica and Sam.

Peter never quite knew how much money there was in any of his businesses. He had only a rough sense of how much inventory his franchises needed or how much the plumbing company would need if Sam wanted to scale. He didn't know how much was going to come in each month or how much his various entities would fall short of profitability. His financial strategy, so far as it existed, was all reactive—anytime he found a hole, he plugged it with the profits he was earning elsewhere.

This was understandably less than ideal to his children, who were trying to build their own careers up within the company.

It didn't have to be this way. He could have explained the costs of equity up front to Jessica and Rich. He could have tracked growth for the plumbing business and tied that to the equity they earned, incentivizing them to focus more on the plumbing business and less on their hardware store ventures.

With a stronger command of his financial numbers, he could have also put all of this in writing. I tell my clients all the time, "If it is not in writing, it did not happen." Documenting decisions and expectations is one of the easiest ways to avoid unmet expectations. It also forces clarity of thinking and commitment when you have to document these things. But this would only have been possible for Peter if he had those numbers to put down on the page.

Once Sam took over, Peter could have explained how much he'd be taking from plumbing and for how long. He could have set up a system to reward Sam for running the company well—perhaps a similar equity deal to the one he intended to offer Jessica and her husband.

All of the numbers he needed to do this were knowable. In fact, most of them appeared on the statements he was getting each month from his accountant.

Simply knowing these numbers and what they meant would have given him clarity that might have removed many of the complaints his children were bringing to him.

Of course, knowing his numbers was no guarantee that Jessica and Rich would focus on plumbing over their other ambitions or that Sam could be calmed as his profits were shifted temporarily, but it certainly would have helped. Everything is always easier when people know where they stand—particularly where they stand financially.

This is an incredibly common situation in family business because, as the great business author Michael Gerber has pointed out, founders are usually technicians instead of business owners. The business grows due to the founder's skills, not because of any deep knowledge of business fundamentals. Many family businesses therefore reach a point when the family in the business wants answers to financial questions and the founder can't provide them.

The language of business is money, and many family business founders are far from fluent. They know how to do the work that brings money in, but they don't know how to manage the money once it's in the company.

If this is true of your business, it's time to brush up on your accounting skills and get answers to those tough family financial questions.

EXIT HOPEVILLE

Being able to explain numbers to family is a great reason to become more fluent in financial statements, but there are other, equally important reasons to focus on this topic. In the first place, you need to understand the key numbers in your business every time you make a big decision. Every major company you've ever heard of makes their decisions work on paper before they make them work in the real world. Otherwise, you are just living in "Hopeville," hoping everything works out somehow. Seldom does that happen.

Any time you go to a bank for a loan, they work the numbers out on paper first. They figure out how likely you are to pay everything back, how long it will take you to pay them back, and how much they'll make on that loan. If the numbers don't work, they don't make the loan.

Walmart doesn't break ground on a new store until they know how much business they can expect, what the labor market looks like in that area, and how long before they break even on the costs of opening their doors.

You should be running your business in the same way. You

should run the numbers on paper for every big decision, avoiding costly mistakes before you make them. If Peter had just done the math on his new hardware store franchises, he might not have invested so heavily up front. Along with reducing his financial exposure, that would have saved him a huge headache with Sam.

Any plan not documented is a dream. It is not a plan.

In 2001, I joined a "dot-com" company. The founder had raised five million dollars in seed capital based on an idea. The cost to build out the infrastructure, hire the team, and purchase the first round of inventory ate up most of the investment. We spent money with the expectation that we would be able to raise more when we needed to. This thinking was the foundation of the dot-com crash in 2000–2001. Many dot-coms had built their business with a focus on growth versus profits. Many never achieved profitability. Most that did not ended up being purchased or shut down.

Ever heard of pets.com? It was a website that sold pet supplies. The company was big enough that it advertised at the Super Bowl and Macy's Thanksgiving Day Parade. But they never proved their viability as a business. Once they ran out of road in Hopeville, there was nowhere else to go. You don't want to run your own business that way.

ANSWER THE BIG QUESTIONS

This clarity isn't just valuable when planning to scale. It can answer some very fundamental questions for you. For instance, is this business of yours viable? In other words, can you make a profit here?

In Mike Machalowicz's book *Profit First*, he suggests that every business owner should start with the amount of profit they need to make and then work backward to determine how much business they need to generate to gain that profit.

It's hard to overemphasize the value of this lesson. Most businesses fail, and most businesses fail because they don't have the cash to keep the doors open and the lights on.

According to the Bureau of Labor Statistics, about 20 percent of new businesses fail during the first two years of being open, 45 percent during the first five years, and 65 percent during the first ten years. The top reason for this failure is inadequate planning and marketing research. Reason number two is a lack of capital and cash flow issues.

Failure isn't always immediately apparent. When things are good, it may seem like the business can keep running forever. But no business is static. They all operate in cycles—sometimes you are up, sometimes you are down. Growing up on a farm, we had a saying: "Make hay when the sun is shining." You should make money when you have the chance, but you also need to have your finances in order so you can save some for a rainy day—because it will rain someday.

It's important for new businesses to have a solid business plan, sufficient funding, and a clear understanding of their target market in order to increase their chances of surviving and thriving in the long term. So, is your business bringing in more money than it's spending? If it isn't yet, can you see a future when that will be the case?

If you are viable, having a stronger sense of your numbers can answer the next big question: Are you sustainable? Sustainability means you can keep making a profit year over year, and you can keep making enough profit that you can eventually start growing. This requires you to bring in enough revenue that you can start getting some money out of the business, allowing you to hire new people, give others promotions and raises, expand the products you offer, open a new store, and so on. Growth eats cash, so you need to be able to feed your business a lot of it.

Basically, the fundamental questions your business has to answer are: Is this going to work? And can you grow it?

Business leaders need to architect their business to get the results they want. You must make it work on paper before it will work for real. Doing so will give you and the family confidence that they can achieve the promised results.

For that reason, these aren't just great questions you need answered; they're questions your family would like answered as well. No one wants to board a rocket ship destined to crash. Showing them that your moon shot has a good chance of success is important to securing their trust. And trust in family business is invaluable.

TRUST BUT VERIFY

Of course, that trust has to go both ways. That's another benefit to having a firm understanding of the crucial numbers in your business. It allows you to make sure you were right to put your trust in people. As Jack Stack, author of *The Great Game of Business,* says, numbers tell a story about people. You need to know what that story is for each person in your organization.

I know a CEO who used to blindly put his trust in the accountant he hired to run the finances for his company. He trusted her so much, he would sign blank checks and let her fill in the amount. But after we actually cracked the books and looked at them carefully, we discovered she'd taken $65,000 from him over the course of a couple years.

She was very adept at hiding her theft, but she only really got away with it for so long because the CEO didn't know how to review the numbers he was seeing.

With everyone in your family business, you should have a policy of trust but verify. It's the same way you probably raised your kids. You put trust in them to do homework, but you would occasionally "spot-check" to make sure it was getting done. Those same kids—as well as every other employee—need to know they can be spot-checked at any time.

Even your accountant should know that. Gallup has found that CPAs are among the most trusted group of professionals, coming in eighth behind professionals like doctors, attorneys, and clergy. They finished ahead of clergy. That kind of trust means most people just blindly follow the advice they get.

But CPAs, like all the rest of us, are human. They make mistakes. Some years back now, an HVAC company I worked with finished the year with several hundred thousand dollars in the bank. The founder's accountant told him that he had to do something with that money before the year ended to avoid a higher tax bill. So, he went out and bought a couple new trucks for his team.

That sounds like a smart decision, except the CPA didn't understand the seasonality flow of business for that company, and the founder didn't take the time to think things through for himself. That company had a huge, predictable slowing-down period near the end of the year. The money in the founder's account could have been used to pay staff through the slow period. Instead, he had to take a loan out to cover the difference.

I'm not blaming anyone here for this oversight. I've run into the same problem myself. My one-time accountant once told me our company had made $1.3 million in profits. Because of the contracts for my team, that meant I should pay out $400,000 in bonuses, which I promptly did. It was only the week after the checks were in the mail that the accountant called me back and said they'd made a mistake. We actually had a $900,000 loss.

From $1.3 million in the black, I was suddenly $1.3 million in the red—all because I didn't think to really look at the numbers myself. It ended up being a $2.2 million mistake.

THE BIG NUMBERS

If you don't understand all the key numbers in your business, it's time to change that. You don't have to take a course in accounting to master the relationship between these numbers in your company. With just a little work, you can understand what makes these numbers go up and down, and that's more than enough in most cases. So long as you have a good accountant doing the math behind the scenes, a basic understanding allows you to spot-check your business, explain your finances to family, and make those big decisions.

That said, I'm going to claim this part of the book is easy. Undeniably, some of it is somewhat complicated. But you can definitely understand it. In fact, all you need to do is understand all the numbers on three forms you're already getting from your CPA: your P&L (profit and loss) statement, your balance sheet, and your cash flow statement.

Your **P&L**, or **income statement**—they're the same thing—shows **revenues** that are coming in, **expenses**, and **profits**. Those expenses come in two types: your variable costs and your fixed expenses. **Variable costs**, as you might assume, go up and down depending on how much you sell. This can include your social media marketing costs that go up the more people click on your ads to buy your products. It can include the costs for product delivery, sales commissions, and fluctuating costs of raw materials. **Fixed expenses** don't really change that much. These include your biggest expense, labor/payroll, as well as things like insurance, electricity, and rent.

Here are some business fundamentals: a profitable business makes more in revenue than they are spending in expenses. To see how you're doing, you want to focus on your **gross profit** and your **gross profit margin**. The former does this very basic math for you, while the latter turns your profit into a percentage of your overall revenue.

Think of it this way. For every dollar of revenue, perhaps forty-five cents goes to variable costs; another forty cents may go to fixed costs. That leaves fifteen cents gross profit, or a gross profit margin of 15 percent. That's a healthy amount. You want your margin to be at 15 to 20 percent, because you still have to take somewhere around 10 percent to cover taxes and leave a little something for potential growth.

That's a lot of information on this one form, but we're not quite done yet. We still need to work out **EBITDA**—which stands for "earnings before interest, taxes, depreciation, and amortization." This number shows your overall operational efficiency over all the things you can control. There's a lot of fancy accounting that goes into the various elements within EBITDA that you can leave to your accountant, but it's good to keep track of this number, as well as your net profit after you subtract all those elements. Basically, this is what is left after everyone gets paid.

That's all for your P&L. The next form you should pay attention to is your **balance sheet**. This is where you'll find information such as your **assets** (things that could be sold to get money—including your inventory), **liabilities** (loans, debt, prepaid stock, and other things you owe), as well as information on things like the **owner's equity** (the amount that belongs to the owner if they were to liquidate the business). It also includes information on **retained earnings**, which is money carried over from one year to the next.

Understanding that equity would have helped Peter a whole

lot when Jessica was still in the business. He could have known precisely how much he had in the plumbing company and how much he could afford to give away.

Finally, we have the **cash flow statement**. Cash is like oxygen in a business, so there's real value in being able to trace every dollar that comes into your company that is spendable and every dollar that's going out. This form lets you trace your company's overall cash journey through the month. Let's say you begin the month with $10,000 in cash. Over the course of the month, you bring in $20,000 in sales. At that point, you have $30,000.

But then you have your expenses. Perhaps payroll is $10,000, rent is $3,000, the electricity bill costs another $750, and so on. All told, your expenses are $17,000. That means you end the month with $13,000—or the original $10,000 plus another $3,000.

The cash flow statement tells you how **liquid** your business is—or how much cash you have that you could spend without having to sell anything. And it lets you know if you are becoming more liquid or less.

Put all together, these numbers tell the story of your company's overall health. Are you making money? How much does it cost to keep the business running? How much profit are you actually making? If you had to sell everything tomorrow, how much would you actually make? And are you increasing your liquidity month over month?

With these answers, you have a much stronger sense of where your company is today. And that can help you plot a path to where you want to go tomorrow.

PROJECTING FORWARD

I know your head might be swimming. These are obviously quite complex numbers, but for now, all you need is a general sense of them. There's value in a deeper education, but at the very least, you should understand what each number tells you about your business.

Once you can do that, you can start taking those numbers and looking toward the future, using budgets, dashboards, and forecasts.

BUDGETS

This is the most basic form of forward planning. On a month-to-month basis, you can give your dollars a home before the new month begins.

Through budgeting, you know how much you need in each business and each department. This was Peter's problem with Sam. He was struggling to budget for his inventory at the franchises. Since he never had the right amount of stock in place, he had to pull money mid-month to cover more shipments. Better budgeting could potentially remove the entire issue with Sam and the plumbing company. At very least, it would have made those transfers more predictable.

There tends to be a negative bias around budgets. Many founders assume they imply constraints. In reality, they represent nothing more than a plan. According to Dave Ramsey, this is really just giving your money a home before the month begins.

You can develop a budget simply by keeping track of the numbers on those statements. You'll eventually see trends in how much money and resources are required for your average April or August.

These trends can allow you to prepare for the next April and the next August. At that point, you can put enough aside for those future costs, creating more certainty about how much you have left to invest in other areas.

DASHBOARDS

With these numbers in hand, you can also focus on the most critical numbers driving your business. These are the numbers that determine whether you're successful or not.

This is a little different than whether you're profitable or not. Here, we're looking more at your sales than your revenue, profits, and losses.

Every company has a **widget**—this is the thing that you sell that drives your revenue. For you, a widget might be service calls. It could be the number of pens you sell. It might be apps downloaded or cars sold. It could be the number of customers or appointments you have.

Your dashboard should keep track of the number of widgets you're selling. It should also track critical numbers associated with the delivery of your widgets. What are the costs involved in making each sale, and are those costs low enough that you remain profitable?

These widget numbers will be different for every business because widgets are based on different business strategies. For instance, in my printing company, our dashboard tracks the number of orders instead of number of customers. Our costs are lower if we have more orders from fewer customers, so we concentrate on maintaining and building on that number.

And this insight is key to becoming more forward looking in your company. Once you have a dashboard in place—along with budgets and all your key numbers—you can start looking at strategy.

In our printing company, since we want more orders and larger orders instead of more new customers, we focus on strategies like bundling that would increase order size and provide a good enough deal that the customers we already have keep coming back. This is the McDonald's Happy Meal dynamic. By making it cheaper and more appealing to get a full meal with a little toy, McDonald's increases the size of its average order. One of our most important goals in recent years has been to boost our average order size to $200 by bundling products together.

Instead of having to deliver four products separately—cutting our profit margin extremely low—we could deliver four products at once, save our customers money, and make far more ourselves.

FORECASTING

This leads us into forecasting, or as I like to think of it, the "what if" games. In the words of author and consultant Peter Drucker, repurposing a line from none other than Abraham Lincoln, "The best way to predict the future is to create it." That's what the "what if" game allows you to do.

What if you open another store? What if the cost of your products goes up? What if you hire five more people? What if you bundle your products together? What if you start selling a new product? What if rent increases?

With the numbers you now have in hand, you can answer these questions with reasonable accuracy. You can know the costs, the resources you have to allocate, and what you need to happen in order to continue to achieve a profit.

I recommend a three-year forecast. That's far enough out that you can make significant shifts to create that future but close enough that you can take the concrete steps now to start making it happen.

And that, for a family business founder, is really the whole financial ball game.

CREATING ROOM FOR STRATEGY

Alan Miltz is a bestselling author. He made his career advising companies on how to understand cash in their business. He's developed this concept, the power of one, that suggests companies can make huge amounts of profit simply by moving the needle 1 percent in a few key areas. If you increased revenue 1 percent, cut costs 1 percent, increased your margins by 1 percent, and so on, how much difference would that make to your business?

A lot.

But to do that requires a deep understanding of your finances—and something else: strategy. Once you understand the numbers at the heart of your business, so much more becomes possible. You can grow the way you want to grow, and you can help your family grow into the business.

That's where Peter has landed. He's trying to train not just himself but Sam in the family business numbers. That way, they can both make better business decisions. And they can both begin to plot a strategy that takes care of all of their needs in the future.

CHAPTER 5

STRATEGY

GUY IS THE FOUNDER OF A HUGE PLUMBING BUSINESS. BUT that's not what he set out to do. He started out as a master plumber who wanted to run things his way. He was good at his job and good with his customers, and he wondered why he should give a percentage of the money he made to someone else. So he founded his own company where he controlled what he did and what he made.

Then the predictable thing happened. Guy got busy. And then he got too busy. After a while, there was more demand than he could possibly deliver on his own. He had to put customers off for days because he just couldn't get to every job.

So he hired Evan as an apprentice, and he asked his wife, Jane, to take on some of the accounting and back-office work. Things stabilized for a bit. Since Evan was just an apprentice, at first he acted as a gofer, running errands. With Jane and Evan's help, Guy could focus on work and just about get through all his projects.

But then the company just kept growing. Evan became a journeyman, and Guy started handing him projects. Evan proved to be a good plumber who was also good with the customers. More customers kept calling. Jane took on more admin work, even though she wasn't trained for it. The phone kept ringing.

Before Guy knew it, he had to add another plumber and another truck, and then another of each—until he had six trucks and as many plumbers on his team.

Word of mouth just kept growing. One day, Guy woke up and realized he wasn't really a plumber anymore; he was a businessman. His days weren't spent fixing leaks, they were spent finding someone to fill in on a job or handling customer complaints. He was doing sales more than he was installing toilets.

Jane wasn't happy; Guy wasn't happy. But he just kept going. One day, one of Guy's contacts asked if he was interested in branching out beyond residential work and taking on a commercial contract installing plumbing for a new strip mall. It was a lucrative job, and Guy had never turned down a good job yet. So he took it. It was only after he'd agreed that he discovered all the red tape and complications that came with commercial work.

It was at that point that Jane threw up her hands. After being roped into the administration of the family business, she'd done as well as she could to train herself for work she hadn't wanted to do in the first place. She was already overwhelmed. Now she was being asked to figure out all the paperwork for commercial plumbing.

In the midst of a fight with Guy, she asked him, "Is this even something you want to do? Is this even the company you want to run?"

That stopped Guy in his tracks—because he couldn't honestly say yes anymore.

DECIDE WHERE YOU WANT TO GO

Strategy is the number one reason founders come to me. So many of them find themselves in Guy's situation. They start a family business because they're good at what they do, and they want to be their own boss. When you start a business, you take whatever work comes your way. At some point, though, you realize you've lost control of your own company. You don't know where you're headed or why you're heading that way.

It's easy to get lost like that when you're a technician who is suddenly expected to understand management, leadership, finance, and strategy. These are things no one ever taught most founders.

Guy moved from unclogging drains and installing water heaters himself to supervising that work. Then, he took on commercial plumbing jobs not because it was what he wanted but because someone offered him the contract. There was no planning involved. There was no strategy. He'd become a passive leader, taking whatever he was offered.

This can lead to all kinds of family issues. Jane's situation is as common as Guy's. She came in to run the office temporarily when things got too busy. But there was never a strategy to transition her back out of the business or to train her for her various new roles. She simply did whatever new work came into the office.

A lack of strategy in a company creates confusion about the future. No one knows what the business is supposed to look like in a year, so no one knows what their role should look like. Without that clarity, fights and misunderstandings are inevitable.

The inverse is also true, though. The clearer your strategy, the more settled everyone can be in the business. The more they'll know what tomorrow looks like and where they want to fit in that tomorrow.

HOW DO YOU WIN?

Clear strategy offers another major benefit to the family business. It makes it clear how the company is going to win. And winning solves a lot of issues. If you have two children in the business with one higher up the leadership tree and making more than their sibling, that's a recipe for a lot of family business chaos. But it's much less of a problem if everyone is doing well. If the pay difference is not $45,000 over $30,000 but $180,000 over $160,000, there's less room for argument. If everyone is moving the company toward greater success, they're going to be happier in their individual roles.

But that's only possible with a clear strategy. Everyone has to be aiming toward some goal in order to achieve it. I often talk to founders about the purpose of their business. What are they aiming for? What does winning look like for them? Unfortunately, sometimes, the answers show no thought has really been put into this subject at all. More often than you might imagine, the answer I receive is that the company's purpose is to make more money. And that's it.

But no one wants to work for a company whose sole goal is to enrich the founder. Your employees don't want to work to make you money. And your kids and other relatives don't want to do that either. You can understand why Jane might feel particularly aggrieved at spending years in administration just so Guy could keep making more money. Even though she got to enjoy those benefits, it offered no motivation to keep going into the office.

You have to offer people more than that. You need a path forward that leads in a direction everyone wants to go. That's the essence of strategy.

Instead of remaining stuck in "startup mode" forever, where you're still trying to prove viability and sustainability, strategy can give you purpose and a way to win that makes everyone happy. In those early months, you do have to do whatever is possible to show the company is profitable sustainably. But if the numbers we covered in the last chapter show your business has passed that hurdle, you can move into scaling strategically. Instead of trying to do everything, working long hours seven days a week while trying to be a manager and a technician, you can grow in the way you want to go.

Put simply, if you are viable and sustainable, you don't have to chase every dollar. You can chase the dollars you want to chase. And when you get those dollars, you—and everyone in the family—can win.

WHAT DOES WINNING REALLY LOOK LIKE?

But that's only part of a winning picture. To really sketch out what winning looks like for your company, you have to provide everyone with three things: a mission, a purpose, and a vision.

These are often misunderstood concepts and become interchangeable to founders, but each one serves a different purpose. Your mission answers two questions: what will we do and how will we do it? A core purpose explains why you are doing this at all. And your vision is a picture of the reality you want to create.

Let's take these one at a time, starting with your mission. Here, you have to start by asking the right questions.

Some of these questions are basic and fundamental. For instance, what are your products and services? What is it, exactly, that your company sells? This may seem obvious to you, but Guy let that answer get away from him. He didn't want to install commercial plumbing. The services he intended to provide all involved residential plumbing.

Once you know what you're selling, you should ask yourself where you want to play. How big a territory do you want to cover? Do you want to live and work in the city? Do you want to be out in the country? Do you want to be all over? Are you aiming to cover a suburb, a state, or an entire region? What do you want your company's reach to look like?

Or, to refine these a bit, A.G. Lafley and Roger Martin lay out in their book *Playing to Win* five basic questions you have to answer about your business:

1. What are our winning aspirations?
2. Where will we play?
3. How will we win?
4. What capabilities do we have or need?
5. What management systems do we need?

You don't always have to choose the biggest answer to these questions. Take the question "where will we play?" I've worked with companies that are the main service provider for their small city. I know founders who are the biggest name for a large number of rural counties far from the bigger players in the city. Knowing where you want to do your work can set necessary boundaries on your scaling. If you don't want to be driving three hours away to a job, don't take that work. If you don't want to sit in city traffic, stick with a more rural scope.

Along with these questions, let's ask another big one. This is your main financial question: how much do you want to make? When you have that figure, you can set it as your target and work backward. That's how the NFL sets salary for players. They know they have a certain amount of money, and they work backward from their priority players on down.

You should aim to have a certain amount coming in, a certain amount you'll keep, and a certain amount you're paying everyone else. If you reach that target, you don't have to keep taking more work, particularly if it falls outside the products and services you normally offer and the area you want to work in.

Answering these questions helps you get a sense of the capabilities you need to be in place in order to win. You can start to create a picture of those capabilities and when you need them ahead of time. If Guy wanted to be the biggest plumbing company in his area, he might need five trucks and five plumbers. But he might not need the sixth one. Knowing those needs ahead of time can allow you to begin to chart your strategy.

WORKING YOUR CORE

Strategy touches on more than the general direction you want to go and the limits you want to put on your growth. It also involves what you want your company to stand for. And to answer that, you have to answer some questions about your core.

We start with your core purpose. What is it that you're doing to make a difference? As Steve Jobs put it, how are you going to "make a dent in the universe"?

This is where we get away from that surface-level answer of wanting to make money and go deeper. In my coaching business, for instance, my core purpose is to make a significant impact on the people I interact with. I know that I have the skills and knowledge to help guide family business founders to more peace in the family and prosperity in the office. That's why I do what I do.

But that isn't why you do what you do. That's unique to you.

I worked with a home builder whose purpose was not just to build homes but to change lives by helping people achieve the American dream. Everyone wants a place they can call their own, and his company helps people do that.

Guy's purpose was to make sure people had the water and

heat to make their lives comfortable and safe within their own homes. That last work is key. Knowing that core purpose, it was clear that Guy shouldn't be doing commercial work. He cared about helping people in their *homes*.

With your core purpose in hand, you can ask another core question: what are your core values? Essentially, how are you going to play this game? How will you treat employees? How do you treat your customers? How do you treat your vendors?

This is where you set the behaviors you want to see across your business. Setting this down creates a benchmark. People know what's expected of them when they come to work for you. Family members know what's expected if they join the business.

The next core question is who your core customer is. Create a profile of them. What are their needs? What are their challenges and desires? How does your company and your products or services meet those needs? What kind of customer experience do you want to offer them? You need to know your customer's PICW: problems, issues, challenges, and wants.

And crucially, what is your brand promise to them? Do you want to be known for the quality of your work? The efficiency? The value? You may strive for perfection in all these areas, but you're likely only going to be known for one. Walmart, for instance, does care about customer service, but they're known for the value they offer their customers. They have the cheapest products around. It's why they name their generic products Great Value. Nike tries to offer value for its shoes, but they're known for their expensive, quality designs.

Don't underestimate the value of your brand. People often make purchasing decisions based solely on what they think of a company's brand. For instance, if you go to Walmart and look at the sugar selection, you'll find the Walmart Great Value sugar right next to the Imperial Sugar brand. In all likelihood, both bags of sugar came from the same plant using the same sugar cane and same process. The Great Value price will be significantly lower than the Imperial Sugar price. And yet, people still buy Imperial Sugar. The only reason to do so is because they associate the brand's name with quality.

McDonald's is the world's largest fast-food chain. We all know it isn't because they have the best-tasting burgers in the world. Instead, the brand is associated with speed, dependability, and affordability. Anywhere in the world, you can go to a McDonald's, and you know you'll get a Big Mac at a good price that tastes just like it does at home—and you know you'll get it in a matter of minutes. It is all about consistency.

My next-door neighbor owns three McDonald's franchises. One day, during one of our regular conversations at the fence, I asked about how he ran them.

"Wait right here," he said. He returned a moment later with two four-inch-thick binders.

"This is the operating system for McDonald's. We can't deviate from this one iota. If we do, they can pull our franchise."

That's the level of consistency McDonald's demands.

Knowing the core of your brand allows you to communicate in your advertising and live it in your business. It can grow out of your core purpose and core values that you aim at your core customer. If you know who you want to serve, how you want to serve them, and why you want to serve them, you can build a brand around those realizations.

But that is only part of the value here. Knowing your core allows you to understand what you're doing in this business. And writing all of these elements of your core out allows everyone else to understand the same thing. Your customers, your employees, your family, and yourself: everyone will know what this company is all about.

EATING THE ELEPHANT

With all this new understanding of your company, you can now build a strategy that leads your company into the future you want—serving the customers you want from the purpose you want and reaching the profits you want.

In other words, you can create what Jim Collins has called a "Big Hairy Audacious Goal," or BHAG—or as I like to call it, the ten-year vision. One of my jobs as a coach is to help companies create a ten-year vision. This is your overriding purpose. According to Collins, it's a "clear and compelling" message that is immediately understood, like NASA shooting for the moon.

To understand the value of a ten-year vision, think of running your business like putting together a jigsaw puzzle. I like to do these in my downtime, and I sometimes challenge myself to do one without looking at the picture on the box. However, it's much faster and easier to use that picture. That's what your ten-year vision is—it's the picture that helps you assemble all the pieces.

To accomplish your ten-year vision, you have to break strategy down into ever smaller parts. This is sometimes called "eating the elephant." The only way to eat an elephant—a huge, daunting task—is one bite at a time.

Let's start with the whole, big elephant. For this, you need to build out a ten-year vision. Look in your crystal ball and see your ideal business future in ten years. Taking into consideration all the points we've covered in this chapter, write down what this company looks like. What region is it serving? What does its brand look like? How much money is it bringing in?

That's where you want to steer this company. But it's hard to steer successfully when your only target is so far out. So the next step is to break this down into a three-year plan. Where do you need the company to be in three years in order to be on course for that ten-year vision? At this point, we bring in the financials we covered in the last chapter. Based on your numbers today, what would they need to look like in order to afford the changes necessary to be about a third of the way to your goal in three years' time? How much do you need to make to make these changes and stay profitable?

Usually, there are multiple answers here. Your aim should be to choose the best option. In my printing company, to get to the size I'm aiming for in ten years, I need either a second machine or three new employees. Both will cost me about $200,000 over that period. But bringing in three new people can lead to a lot of problems. I'd have to deal with turnover and sick days and so on. With that in mind, it's far better value to simply buy a new machine.

This demonstrates my second favorite word, "leverage." The definition of leverage is something you build once but use many times over. Technology is an obvious example here, as is the printing machine. That machine fits the criteria for investment. You should only invest in something if it makes you money, saves you money, or gives you a competitive advantage. The printing machine will both save us money and give us an advantage.

But even if it's the right call, that decision leads to secondary problems. Our location can't hold a second printing machine. So we would have to move to a new space, which would add $3,000 a month in rent. That complicates the math. In the end, we can afford those extra costs because we still feel we get more value from the second machine. But that may not be the call you make.

Once you do make that kind of call, though, it's time to shrink your timelines further. Next up, let's consider what needs to happen over the next year for you to be heading directly for that three-year goal. With that target in place, you can break things down to the smallest level and set quarterly goals to hit that annual target.

At this point, eating the elephant should feel much more achievable. You can set deliverables for the end of each quarter over the next year and tie those deliverables to the numbers you need to see. The path you follow to those numbers should form the center of your strategy.

WHERE DOES EVERYONE FIT?

With a clear strategy, you can answer a lot of the questions family and employees might have for you in the business. You can tell them where the company is going. You can tell them why the company does the work it does.

And importantly, you can begin to figure out where each person best fits. When you have a strategy in place, it's far easier to see who has the right skills for each function in the business. Jane may not have wanted to work in admin, but she may find she has the aptitude for marketing. Evan may be ready to move into an oversight position, allowing Guy to spend more time on higher-level problems.

Those changes would serve strategy while also giving everyone a place they belong in the company. As we will soon see, clarity of roles and responsibilities is critical to family-business success.

In other words, understanding strategy creates the opportunity to understand where each person fits in the functions of your company—and that will drive you toward your long-term goals with greater purpose and fulfillment for all parties.

CHAPTER 6

REVIEWING FUNCTIONS

I WORK WITH A PROMOTIONAL FAMILY BUSINESS RUN BY two brothers. They specialize in putting logos on hats, shirts, and mugs, as well as awards-show items. Phil, the older brother, is the CEO. Bill is head of sales. To put it very bluntly, neither is suited to their role.

Phil is great with financials, but he struggles with things like strategy. He is one of those CEOs I mentioned in the last chapter who insist that the core purpose of the company is just to make more money. He can't see beyond the value of making profit. Purpose makes no sense to him if he can't attach a dollar sign to it.

Meanwhile, Bill is extremely analytic, but he's not a people person. He is great with organizing processes but can't hold a conversation for more than a few minutes. He has a slightly standoffish personality. None of this is good news when you have to work in sales. It's perhaps the most people-facing role in the company.

Neither Phil nor Bill is a bad fit for the company itself; they just don't belong in the roles they currently have. Phil's financial focus would be great if he had Bill's role. Having a primary motivation of just generating more money is exactly what you want from your head of sales. It's just not the right attitude from a CEO. Likewise, Bill's analytical skills would be perfect in operations or metrics, where he wouldn't need to interact with a lot of people each day.

Simply finding the right function to fit each person could make all the difference. We have to help each person find their chair. When someone doesn't have a chair, they don't know what to do. They just wander, getting into everybody else's business, trying to find a place. In different roles, they might find they really excel. Instead of constantly feeling like they're grinding, they could come to a point where they enjoy what they're doing. And that would benefit the family and the business.

THE DANGERS OF A POOR FIT

We've all had jobs we didn't feel we were right for. When I worked for my dad at his service station, the work didn't interest me. It didn't fit my skillset or offer me the kind of purpose I was looking for. When you look at it from that perspective, it's hardly surprising I took the first opportunity I got to move on.

And that's what you can expect from the family members in your business if their roles don't match their interests or talents.

A lack of alignment here can also lead to a lot of friction. You want the right people in the right departments so they can live up to the responsibilities you set for them. But if a natural introvert is in charge of sales, they can fall short of those responsibilities. They can also begin to clash with others in the organization who are putting pressure on them. That head of sales might get into fights with whoever is running finances for the company. Or the family member in charge of sales may seek to deflect blame and get angry at the forgetful member of the family who's in charge of inventory.

Along with all the drama, this inevitably slows growth and weakens efficiency, harming your strategy and risking all the issues that we discussed in the last chapter when failing to win.

If you want to avoid those risks, you need to understand the functions within your business, who fits where, and create a people system that allows everyone to flourish while fulfilling their responsibilities.

YOUR PROACTIVE BUSINESS PLANNING AND EXECUTION SYSTEM

To find the proper fit for everyone in your organization, you first need to create a Proactive Business Planning and Execution System for your business. Luckily, every system involves the same eight foundations.

FOUNDATION #1: LEADERSHIP

At the top, you have your **leadership** function. This includes the CEO and other executive roles. Leadership is primarily tasked with captaining the ship. They determine the strategy and core values. They break down what makes the company different from its competitors and tell everyone where the company is going.

FOUNDATION #2: MARKETING

The second function is **marketing**. In modern business, marketing has three legs: attracting customers, nurturing customers, and attracting talent. The first leg, *attracting customers*, is the one you probably associate with marketing. This includes all the efforts required to share your brand and bring customers to your company. But marketing also *nurtures* the customers you have by keeping your company top of mind when they need your products or services again.

Finally, marketing is the function responsible for *attracting potential new employees*. In times with low unemployment, this is a particularly valuable use of marketing to ensure you get the people you need to scale your business—as we'll discuss more in a moment.

FOUNDATION #3: SALES

Next up, we have **sales**. This one probably seems pretty self-explanatory. Sales is tasked with taking someone from being interested to becoming a customer. But there's more to it than that.

Sales is a process, one that I like to call R2D3. You can think of it as the *Star Wars* character R2D2's little brother. The first "R" stands for *relationship*. People do business with people they know, like, and trust. That requires a relationship. The second "R" is for *rapport*. This means your salespeople need to build more than just any relationship, they need to create one in which a potential customer feels close enough and comfortable enough that they trust your company.

The first "D" stands for *discovery*. Essentially, a salesperson's job is to discover the PICW of their potential customer. As you may recall from our discussion in Chapter 5, PICW stands for problems, issues, challenges, and wants. You should know these for your company. Now, you need your sales team to discover them for your customer. They also need to discover answers to four additional questions:

1. Are they talking to the decision maker?
2. Is there a clear issue or problem to be solved?
3. Is the customer ready to do something about it?
4. Do they have a budget for the solution?

Knowing the PICW and these additional four pieces of information allows sales to move to the next "D" in the process: *design*. People really don't care what you or your product can do. They care about getting a solution to their problem. Designing a solution based on discovery ties your company's solution directly to their PICW. This step usually involves a presentation or proposal to demonstrate the solution. Using what sales pros call trial closes, sales can validate that the customer understands how your solution can solve their problem.

The final "D" is for *decision*. Sales and the prospect need to decide to move forward or delay a decision based on situational factors. No matter what, some sort of decision has to be made.

I lay this all out here in order to show that sales is much more than just cold-calling potential customers and trying to get a sale. There should be a whole process behind it—and people expert in following that process to success.

FOUNDATION #4: OPERATIONS

So far, we've covered the obvious functions, but **operations** may not be quite so obvious for many founders. This is where you cover delivering products and services, ensuring quality, and making sure everything is done as efficiently as possible. Essentially, it's everything that goes into sales from a prospect to a customer.

Operations is where process becomes your friend. Having clear processes to deliver your product or service creates predictability and quality. It gives you confidence that you can deliver what you sold with a high degree of customer satisfaction.

Operations also cover purchasing and inventory. Some of these responsibilities can have huge ramifications for your business. You don't want to carry more inventory than sales can support. This is often where some of those numbers we covered in Chapter 4 can move in the wrong direction. If you remember Peter's difficulty reaching profitability with his franchise stores, it all came down to inventory.

FOUNDATION #5: CUSTOMER EXPERIENCE

Customer experience is the function that most businesses ignore or take for granted. In my experience, this is the function most of my clients have failed to focus enough attention on. This is a mistake. Customer experience should be the best source for new business for your company. This is no exaggeration. By my estimations, 50 percent of all new business should come from your existing customers. If that isn't the case at your company, look at your customer experience function.

Those responsible for this work manage your ongoing customer relationships. They measure satisfaction, gather feedback, stay in touch, and see if your current set of customers will refer you to the next ones. If you're falling short, review the processes in this function and figure out how to deliver a wow experience such that your customers would be willing to recommend you to other people they know.

FOUNDATION #6: TEAM MEMBER EXPERIENCE

Your **team member experience** function is essentially your People department. It's how you hire, manage, and take care of the people working for you. They recruit and onboard new team members. They develop your team and handle compensation, corrective action, and exiting people in the company. This is an incredibly important function in your company, as your team member experience function will be responsible for how your people fit into the company, which we'll discuss more in a moment.

FOUNDATION #7: SYSTEMS AND PROCESSES

Systems and processes are responsible for all the systems necessary to run the business. They maintain your financial systems, your ERP, inventory systems, and so on. This is where you implement and maintain supporting processes for HR, accounting, legal, and IT. They handle your software and hardware needs as well as many communication needs, such as meetings and quarterly and annual planning.

FOUNDATION #8: METRICS

Finally, we have **metrics**. Here, we find the function responsible for all those important numbers we covered in Chapter 4. In metrics, you'll design your dashboards where you'll find those core numbers that tell you if you're winning or not.

Needless to say, your financials are some of the most important metrics we need to know to make good business decisions. They aren't the only ones, though. Using the right metrics, for instance, you can also determine the effectiveness of your sales function and push for improvements.

Metrics also includes all that information on your widgets. Essentially, metrics tell you if you're accomplishing what you need to accomplish. This is how you keep score and make sure your company is still winning.

Every company needs to maintain all eight functions to be successful. These may look very different for a startup than they do for a thousand-person corporation, but they all have to be tended to by the people in your business.

WHEN TO WEAR MULTIPLE HATS

In larger companies, there are multiple people fulfilling each of these functions. There are many jobs that fall under each function, creating lots of possibilities for every family member, as well as for all your other employees.

However, for smaller businesses, it's very likely that you and perhaps some members of your family have to wear multiple hats across the business. The person running systems may also run metrics. Leadership may also be the entire sales department.

However, this should ideally be a temporary measure. There's real value in people specializing in their function. Specialization allows each person to focus on what they can do best for the business. Spreading yourself—or anyone—across multiple functions in a larger organization won't allow you to focus on all the responsibilities in that function.

There's also value in keeping functions separate to keep everyone honest. There's a thing called the fraud triangle. The three corners are opportunity, incentives, and justification. The more your company creates space for any of these three, the more likely some employee will be tempted to commit fraud. Stealing and other bad behavior in a business often starts small. Someone steals a box of pens because they feel like they aren't being paid enough. When they aren't caught, they escalate to ever higher acts of theft.

Developing a better strategy helps reduce justification and the incentives to begin stealing, but by keeping functions separate, you limit opportunity and increase the control you have over your finances, thus closing every angle of the fraud triangle.

BUILDING YOUR TEAM MEMBER EXPERIENCE FUNCTION

In order to fill all your functions effectively, you'll need an effective people system. A people system includes all the various processes that touch the people in your company—from hiring people to training people and letting them go.

This is a vast process, but here, we can highlight some of the major elements you'll need in your family business people system.

CREATE FUNCTIONAL ACCOUNTABILITY

Before you do anything, you need to add to the clarity you've achieved in your functions by creating structure around responsibilities. To do this, you should take a page out of Brad Smart's book, *Topgrading*, and write **role scorecards** for every position within your organization. Scorecards allow you to set expectations for each role. What skills do your people need? What are they responsible for?

In addition to Smart's basic role scorecard, I recommend you add in other elements of your business here, such as alignment with core values, the level of authority associated with the position, and individual development goals.

We're going to need these scorecards in a moment, so keep them close. In the meantime, though, you can move on to **developing your employee policies.** Think back to your core values. How do you expect employees to behave? What is the consequence of failure to meet those standards?

Codify all of this in a **team member handbook.** This is different from a playbook, which explains how all the processes in your company work. In contrast, a handbook contains all the policies that undergird your company. Crucially, when this is complete, make sure every employee signs off that they received it. This can offer you some real protection down the line. I once hired someone who requested two weeks' paid time off around Thanksgiving when they were only two months into the job. His family had planned a nice vacation in Florida over that period, and he understandably wanted to join them.

Unfortunately, we couldn't make this work. I let him know that time off didn't kick in until an employee had been with the company for a year. And our business stayed open over Thanksgiving week. I tried to compromise and give him a week off, but he didn't accept and left the company.

That should have been it, but later, I found out he intended to file a discrimination lawsuit against my business. It turned out he was gay (which I did not know until that point), and he accused my company of denying him time off because of that. Luckily, he had signed off on our handbook of policies, which stated very clearly he wasn't entitled to paid leave. That saved us from a potentially costly and embarrassing case.

Hopefully, you never face that kind of situation. But even if you don't, a handbook and a role scorecard are great first steps toward clarifying exactly what is expected of everyone who works in your business.

EVALUATE YOUR TEAM

Now, grab those role scorecards you've set down nearby. We're going to use them to evaluate your staff. You want to break everyone in your organization down into four categories. First, you have your **A-players**. These are the people in your organization who are highly aligned with your values and really perform. Ideally, you want 70 percent of your company to be A-players. If you're below that number, it's a priority to bring more A-players in. For the A-players you already have, focus on asking them what they need from you. What can you do to help them perform at an even higher level? What can you do to make this job more enjoyable for them?

Next up are your **B-players.** These individuals have high alignment with your values, but their performance is lower than you'd like. These people have every chance of becoming A-players, they're just lacking the right tools to hit all your expectations. Here, you should concentrate on providing training to improve their performance.

The third category includes all your **B/C-players.** These people are high performers with low alignment to your company values. These players are really on the margin. Look for tools to correct their behavior to try to improve those alignment numbers. If they can't improve, though, you may want to consider downgrading them to the final category.

That's where you find your **C-players.** These workers score poorly on alignment and performance. You should aim to remove all of them from your organization. Whether you can let them go today or in six months may depend on circumstances, but they aren't offering you enough to be worth holding onto longer term.

With clarity on who performs and who believes in your values, you can start to build the team you need to see every function succeeding. And that improves your numbers and allows you to achieve your strategic goals. It also shows everyone in the family where they stand now and what they have to do to become A-players in their own right.

ATTRACT AND KEEP THE RIGHT PEOPLE

To keep your A-players and attract new A-players, you should develop a **compensation philosophy and strategy**. Instead of paying whatever seems right in the moment and raising salaries automatically well beyond the going rate, you should aim to find the right pay point for each position. You need to be able to answer a couple fundamental questions for each position: What is the least you're going to pay? And what's the most you're going to pay?

You don't have to figure this out on your own. Information is available for most jobs online. You can find average pay for positions by industry and by location. Ideally, you want to fall somewhere in the middle of the spectrum. Once you find the right spectrum for your company, stick to it. That will help rein in budgets and keep pay manageable while you negotiate with various A-players.

But you'll still need new talent in your organization. To bring it in, you'll need to build up three operations: **attraction**, **building a virtual bench**, and **strengthening your radar**.

As I said above, **attraction** is part of the marketing function. In today's job market you have to adopt the mindset of a marketer and recruiter. You can't just post a job and hope that you get a good candidate. The best people won't apply because they aren't currently looking for another job. The people you want to hire—those A-players—are working somewhere else. You have to adopt a process of recruiting, very similar to a paid recruiter. You have to advertise to these people. I know many founders feel this is just too much effort. But trust me, I've worked with seven companies named the best place to work in Dallas–Fort Worth, and all of them use marketing tactics to bring in new A-players.

While you're marketing to the top talent in your area, you should aim to **build a virtual bench** of the talent you encounter.

The bench is for people you might not have a position for right now but who would be excellent additions in the future.

I was once at a restaurant where I was served by this incredible server. It wasn't just that he provided fantastic service; he also had what I call the "it" factor. He was so charismatic. After I finished my meal, I asked him if he'd be interested in making more money.

"How much more?" he asked me.

After he told me he made about $35,000 as a server, I told him he could be making $50,000—if he wanted to work for me. Handing him my card, I said, "If you're interested, give me a call."

A short time later, he did call. I hired him immediately. That server went on to become a regional director in my company before being hired away and becoming a VP of national accounts elsewhere. He was an incredible talent, and I would have missed him if I hadn't been aiming to build a bench of talent.

To build that bench, you need to **strengthen your radar** for talent so you always know what's on the horizon. Are you looking for talent in the networking groups and organizations you belong to? Make sure everyone knows that you're always open to reviewing a good résumé.

I once hired a computer programmer from Russia through a recommendation of a colleague. His English was a little rough at the time, but it turned out that he was a world-class programmer.

Knowing about talent and advertising for talent are great ways to start attracting talent to your company. But to really take advantage of this, you have to have a good **hiring system** in place to make sure those people enter the company and enter in the right positions. Far too often the people responsible for hiring aren't actually trained in hiring. They hire the way they were hired. You need to train your people up on a set process. I recommend a three-interview process that starts with a phone screen to check for alignment of values, followed by a competency interview to see if they have the right skills. If the prospect makes it through those two rounds, you can do a job history interview reviewing their relationship to previous managers and companies.

As you interview, be sure to rank results using your role scorecards. Then you should contact your top three candidates—all of them. If your top choice passes, move on to the second choice, and then the third. If none of those three wants the job, instead of going to your fourth choice, just start over. That ensures you keep C-players out of the organization.

ONBOARDING AND FEEDBACK

With new hires coming into the company, be sure to review your role scorecards and set expectations on day one. And don't forget to give each new employee a copy of your employee handbook right away.

From there, you should determine the training necessary for each particular job and set up regular meetings to review comprehension and improvement in the first months of employment.

You also want **a monthly one-on-one meeting** to dig into each new employee's progress and their overall feelings about the organization. This is a nice chance to get some feedback from your future A-players. It's also a good opportunity to sit down with family members new to the business and go over their performance and how well they're integrating into the company.

You can go even further with your check-in meetings by establishing **quarterly feedback sessions** across all teams and running eNPS and engagement surveys to get a picture of operations and where you could most improve. Once a year, you may also want to run a **leadership 360** to get a clear picture of performance for every leader in your organization. These 360s would allow family and other employees to offer feedback to you and other leaders in your organization, making sure their voices get heard.

DEVELOPMENT

Almost every worker is looking to advance in their career. That's especially true of family and your A-players. Develop your systems for raising people up in your organization. Sketch out potential career paths. Consider all the training opportunities you need to provide to those who show the talent to advance.

This is going to be very important later when you carve out a **development plan** for family that allows them to organically rise to the top of the company—as we'll discuss further in Chapter 9. But it's valuable for every employee. While you may particularly want your son or daughter to eventually take over, there needs to be a path to success for everyone in the company.

CORRECTION AND EXIT

Even with great recruiting, training, and opportunities for feedback, you'll still end up with some B/C-players and C-players. It's inevitable. And that means your people system needs tools to correct behavior and, sometimes, to remove employees from the company. For the B/C-players who remain in the company, how many verbal warnings do they get? What does a verbal warning entail?

Whatever decisions you come to here, be sure to be consistent and to document every incident thoroughly. As with your handbook, this can protect you if anyone attempts to argue they were unfairly treated.

After a certain number of warnings, you'll have to be prepared to escalate to termination. This isn't just about telling someone they're fired. You have to have a process in place to determine any severance, removing any security issues (such as changing passwords or getting keys back), and returning company assets. You'll always want to have a process in place to relay the news to the rest of your team.

Everyone should know the path that would lead to termination, and it should be clear to family in the business that they are not exempt from these rules.

Once again, document everything, and where possible, conduct exit interviews to determine the causes that led to this point.

AN ENGINE RUNNING ON FEWER CYLINDERS

Growing up in my family business, we did a lot of work on car engines. In my work as a coach, I've realized that a business is a lot like an eight-cylinder engine. If one cylinder isn't firing, that is going to impact the overall performance of the vehicle. If left unattended, it can do permanent damage to the entire engine.

It's the same with your business. If one function is run poorly, it will affect the entire organization. If one function has family who aren't trained or is full of B/C-players who don't get the core values of the company, it can reduce the success of the entire business. And if you don't repair the damage quickly, it can cause lasting harm to your customers, company, and family.

Attending to each function and building a sturdy, well-thought-out people system will go a long way toward creating long-term stability for your organization.

For most businesses, this is where the advice would end. Get control of your numbers, set strategy, and focus on functions and people. But there are more complex concerns in family business. Now that we have the basic business ideas covered, it's time to turn our attention to the family side of family business.

PART III

FITTING FAMILY IN

CHAPTER 7

SET YOUR PRIORITIES

STACI IS MY ONLY CHILD. I LOVE HER MORE THAN ANYthing. She's smart and very talented, but like many people, it took her a while to figure out what she wanted to do with her life.

When she finished high school, she started college, like most kids do. But she never quite took to her studies. As her academic disinterest became ever more apparent, I kept asking, "What do you want to do?"

She didn't know. She began looking outside of the classroom for inspiration. At one point, she began working with a client of mine, doing graphic design. She met her future husband, Joey, there, who was in production there. She moved out of the family home. When she dropped out of college, I asked if this job was what she really wanted to do.

She still didn't know.

All she knew at that point was that she wanted to make more money. She enjoyed graphic design and was very good at it, but she didn't see a path forward to the income level she wanted to reach—at least not at the place she was working at the time. The problem was that she didn't have any other marketable skills.

In my best coaching mode, I tried to reframe things for her. "If you could do anything in the world, what would you do?"

She told me that she wanted to do hair. She knew some hairdressers could make a pretty decent income, and she liked the idea of the work.

So she went to the top cosmetology school in the Dallas–Fort Worth area. After she graduated with honors, we set up her salon. Once again, she ran into the same trouble. She was good at what she was doing, but it wasn't clear how she'd reach the income level she wanted to hit. She had good word of mouth. We set up a referral program. But she couldn't get her client levels high enough. Eventually, two years in, she burned out.

It was time to start over again. This time, she went back to the one job she'd really liked and excelled at: graphic design. Maybe if she ran her own printing company, she could make enough to build a life with Joey.

The only problem was that she and Joey didn't have the money to start the company. That's where I came in. I was the Bank of Dad. I fronted the cash in exchange for 40 percent of the company.

When Staci balked at her father once again funding her efforts to find her way in the world, I told her I was doing it because supporting her was what it was all about for me. I have been very blessed to have the resources to help. It was an honor, not a requirement. I think a lot of parents feel that way when it comes to their children.

"Look," I told her, "I'm probably going to put half a million dollars into this thing. If it doesn't work out, I'm going to be okay with that. I'd rather eat all these costs than have you be miserable."

Whatever the outcome—whether Staci turned the company into a huge success or walked away in a couple years—I would have been on her side. Because my priority was maintaining that relationship with my daughter. To me, that's always more important than business or money.

WHAT MATTERS MOST?

There's an exercise I like to do with my family business clients. I ask them to write down their top five priorities in order. You can do that too. Take a moment, find a piece of paper, and write down what really matters to you.

Without looking at your list, I bet I can name one item that comes in your top three: family. For many of us, family is what matters most. Family comes first. At least, that's what we tell ourselves.

Unfortunately, many of us don't act like that. When I told Staci I'd eat that $500,000 loss, I meant it—because she is more important to me than business. I know that's probably true for you as well, but often, business stress can cloud our judgment. We're so busy, we need our spouse to keep managing the admin side of things, even if they hate the work. We've sold ourselves on the idea of our kids taking over for so long, we can't accept it when they tell us they want something else for themselves.

We mean to put family first, but we spend all of our time and energy on work instead. Our hearts say family is the top priority, but our actions suggest it's really the business. When our actions are not in line with our priorities, we suffer from guilt and stress. It is not until we straighten those two out that we can begin to see light at the end of the tunnel.

Improving the business side of things will be a major help in creating peace at home and prosperity in the office, but if we really want to disentangle our family business troubles, we have to get those priorities right and put the systems in place that protect family within the business.

DON'T ASSUME

We can start reviewing our priorities by asking a pretty fundamental question: does everyone in the family actually want to be here?

Nick, one of the founders I work with, struggled with this question. He gave all of his children cushy leadership positions in the family car dealerships, but they aren't performing. They seem disinterested in the work. Whether they're handling inventory, managing one of his dealerships, or heading up HR, they're checked out and unmotivated.

He asked me for advice, but before I could give him any, I had a question of my own: "Did you ask if they wanted to work in your company? Did they want those jobs?"

"No," he confessed. "They needed jobs, so I gave them jobs."

Founders often just assume that the family wants to join their successful business. That's the founder's dream—but that doesn't mean that everyone in the family shares that dream.

Instead of building plans based on your assumptions, it's better to give everyone in the family the opportunity to opt out if they want. I've seen the value of providing the space for children to choose their own destinies—even if done reluctantly. Nick did everything he could to keep his kids in his business. However, no matter how much he tried, they ended up walking away, each of them finding their own path.

That's a scary place to put yourself as a founder, but the upside is that allowing family to find their own way ensures everyone who enters the family business wants to be there. They're motivated to work hard, commit, and make the company a success. And everyone who doesn't want to be there is free of resentment. They don't feel forced to stay or feel like they've let anyone down by following their own path.

After a year, Nick finally knew who wanted to be in the company. One of his kids, Matthew, came back now very focused on the car dealership family business. In fact, he was so focused that within three years, he negotiated with his two siblings to buy out their stake and eventually took over the entire company from Nick. Nowadays, he pays his brother and sister a monthly fee for their parts of the business. He'll continue to do so for another eight years. That gives them the money and time they need to explore their own careers while the family business keeps running strong.

Everybody was a winner. But that result was only possible because Nick allowed each of his children to discover where they really belonged.

CONSIDER YOUR PERCEPTIONS

We live in a world full of assumptions. We can't help but make them. After all, we only ever get a portion of the truth. Everyone comes into any given situation with a set of mindsets and beliefs that inform their behavior. One of those assumptions is the one Nick stumbled into: the assumption that all of his kids wanted to be part of the family car dealership business.

But as the founder of a family and a business, it's crucial that you interrogate these assumptions—because the wrong assumptions can lead to very negative consequences.

If you label one of your kids as lazy and the other as clever, you may end up forcing all of their actions to fit into those boxes. And that can lead to a lot of bad decisions and misplaced priorities. It can also lead to the "lazy" kid either deciding to live up to their reputation or rebelling and leaving the family and the business altogether.

To limit these blind spots, you can take a page from Byron Katie in her methodology, The Work. There, she recommends we ask ourselves four questions about every assumption. To rephrase those questions slightly:

- Is it true?
- Are you absolutely sure it's true?
- How would you behave if it were true?
- Who would you be if it were not true?

These questions allow us to interrogate our own certainty about our assumptions regarding family and to consider our behavior and choices if those assumptions were true or not. Such questions force us to take a beat, think through our beliefs, and act with more mindfulness.

That's powerful stuff in a family. As William James, the father of American psychology, is reported to have said, "Human beings, by changing the inner attitudes of their minds, can change the outer aspects of their lives."

If we're really putting family first, we have to be sure we change our "inner attitudes" so we can see our family as clearly as possible for who they really are.

DON'T SPARE THEM

For those children who want to stay in the business, you have to bring some parental insight into your business leadership. At some point, most parents learn that it does no good to try to hide the ugly side of life from their kids. It's our job to show our kids how to deal with that ugly stuff because it isn't going to go away.

The same is true when family enters the business. Founders often instinctively want to take on all the hard parts of running the company themselves. They want to shield those they love from the ugly side of business. They want to share the profits and the opportunities and hide the debts, the late nights, and the tough calls. But that doesn't really serve anyone.

Every business has its plus and minus side. A huge spike in revenues is going to come with an increase in taxes and payroll. Just like understanding numbers, strategy, and functions, everyone in the family business should understand its complexities and headaches. That way, they know why you can't just hand them a $20,000 loan at any time and why they can't always have Fridays off. Understanding business realities reduces that toxic entitlement mindset in which some family members come to feel they're owed a certain amount of money and a certain lifestyle. This entitlement often springs from a lack of understanding the real costs.

Even if your family members aren't entitled, by hiding the downsides of the business, you're setting them up to get burned when they have to take more responsibility later. And that may cost them the company. If they don't understand just how much taxes actually cost or the consequences of raising prices suddenly, they could be blindsided by the reality of business ownership once you eventually step away.

Consider the very unpleasant need to occasionally fire people. Anyone with any sense of empathy finds that act extremely upsetting. I've cried after letting someone go. Your family needs to understand this ugly but necessary side of business. Otherwise, they may never let anyone go because they don't want to have to be the "bad guy."

KNOW YOUR BUSINESS'S LIMITS

Allowing family to choose their own path, checking your assumptions about each family member, and showing them every side of the business can help you prioritize family while running your company. But there's one more important factor to recognize: there's only so much a business can do for your family.

Tim is a founder with two sons. Ben is doing extremely well and moving up the business. Junior is struggling. He isn't struggling because he doesn't care about the work or because he wants to do something else. He's not struggling because Tim makes unreasonable assumptions or hides some of the nastier aspects of running a company. Junior is struggling because of addiction.

Tim doesn't know what to do. He wants to help his son, but the only way he knows how is through the business. He assumes a good job and a steady income is better for Junior than the alternative. But in reality, this only hurts the business and doesn't really help Junior.

Addiction, depression, and other mental health issues are *family problems*. They don't have a business solution. Tim and his wife, Janet, would be better off trying to offer help outside the business setting. Offering Junior a place to stay, paying for him to go to rehab, covering his bills out of their own money while he battles for sobriety—those are all excellent tools at the family's disposal. A job and a steady income aren't going to make a difference.

As an entrepreneur, it's easy to fall into the trap of thinking your business and ingenuity can solve everything. But there are times when you have to accept their limits. This is never easy, but placing family as your priority can allow you to be more open to that truth when you need to hear it.

YOU ARE A PRIORITY TOO

Look back at that list of your top five priorities. Now label how many hours a week you put into each. Most founders fail to put themselves in those five priorities in any capacity, and the amount of time they spend on themselves is worryingly low.

But your health, your happiness, your general well-being: these are all important and deserve to be a priority along with family, business, friends, religion, community, and everything else. If you don't attend to your own needs, you can't guarantee you'll have the energy, focus, and capacity to support all those other priorities.

Ultimately, your life needs balance. You want to be working to live and not living to work. You should be working so you can go out with friends, go on vacations, attend church and social functions, volunteer, and enjoy time with your family. Unfortunately, many family business founders are stuck living to work. The very things we should be living for are the things we sacrifice to run the business.

You can't always take time away from work, but you need to build in time to recharge and time to just have fun. It can only help your family, your business, and every other priority.

One way to create more space for yourself is by reducing the family stress you're seeing in the office. Family always trumps business, but in the office, business has to trump family drama. To ensure that's true in your business, you need to codify the kind of relationship you're going to have with family in the business. And that requires the five keys.

CHAPTER 8

THE FIVE KEYS

DOWN IN HOUSTON, THERE'S A B2B JANITORIAL COMPANY that I've consulted with. Mark owns it, and he does 50 percent of sales. For the rest of the sales, he has a small team. On that team is his son, Tyler. Tyler is a nice kid, but he's an absolute slacker. He slumped his way through college, and when he couldn't find a job to meet his lifestyle expectations, his dad hired him.

The desire to protect his son was understandable, but this has led to all kinds of problems for Mark and his business. In particular, Tyler upset the rest of the sales team with his entitled behavior. The sales process requires one of the salespeople to go out to local businesses and provide them with a quote. Tyler doesn't like doing that. Instead, he stays in the office and follows up on quotes. This results in Tyler getting all the sales—and all the commission—for far less work.

Tyler is now making more than $150,000 a year on minimal work while the company continues to lose its sales talent to rivals.

Luckily, Mark has been so successful at running his company that the company has been able to weather these setbacks, but there's now new trouble on the horizon. The company is about to be acquired by a billion-dollar major player in the industry. Mark has negotiated a contingency to keep Tyler in a job—for three years.

But once those three years are up, it's hard to see any reason the new owners would keep Tyler—or where he would go afterward. As soon as they can get rid of him, they almost certainly will. And that will leave Tyler completely unprepared for work in the real world.

AT WORK, BUSINESS TRUMPS FAMILY

In the last chapter, we discussed how family should be a higher priority than business, but there's a crucial caveat to this point: within the context of business operations, the business has to trump family.

We all want to take care of our family—particularly our kids—but that impulse can work against us if we let it affect our business decisions.

Consider a local interior design business I work with. Carol and Dave built it up from nothing and in the last few years have brought their two sons, Bill and Jack, into the company. The company has a trade show in May that has a huge impact on their revenue. It's so important, they start prepping for it in January. In other words, it's a huge deal for them.

Jack, for some odd reason, planned to go on vacation during the week of the trade show. When Carol confronted him about this, he brushed her off. Carol came to me to look for advice. I gave it to her very simply: either he cancels the trip or he should be out of the company.

That's tough advice for a parent to hear, but if you don't draw a line for family in the business, it can lead to all kinds of problems.

I've seen businesses destroyed by favoritism from the founder, theft by siblings, children demanding more compensation than anyone else, and cousins who refuse to do any work at all.

To avoid these issues, you need a system that allows you to keep family in line when they're in the office—a system that puts business first in the business.

FIVE KEY CHANGES

After the general success of their business and the health and happiness of their family, the central concern of most founders is their ability to connect those two things. They want to tie their family's success to their business success. But as we've seen throughout this book already, tying the two together can create a situation in which success and happiness are actually endangered.

To avoid that, you have to create a system that isolates family issues so they remain with the family. You can do that by introducing the Five Keys to your business organization.

KEY #1: CHECK THE RELATIONSHIP AT THE DOOR

Often, founders bring their kids into the business so they can extend their parental control over their children's lives. This usually isn't a conscious decision, but the effect is the same. Think about it. By hiring our kids, we provide them with the care and support they needed as children. We also maintain the kind of control over their lives we had in their childhood.

This can be comforting for both the child and the parent, but it leads to some very negative issues. Primarily, it enables our children to remain children well into adulthood. They never have to take responsibility for themselves, so they never learn how to do it.

But this doesn't prepare them for a world without your protection. What is Tyler going to do three years after that billion-dollar corporation takes over the family janitorial business? His father thought he was doing Tyler a favor, but by failing to hold Tyler accountable, it left him unprepared for real accountability.

The same thing is true for Carol and Jack. By failing to hold Jack accountable, she's created a scenario in which he feels he has the right to relax during the week that determines the company's entire year.

You don't want to make that mistake with your own kids—or any other relatives in the business. To avoid it, the most important key change you can make is to set a policy to check your relationship at the door. That means no special treatment and no extra exceptions or benefits. If everyone arrives at 9:00 a.m. for work, family arrives at 9:00 a.m. If they arrive at 9:30, you write them up. They get punished the same way as anyone else.

This extends to rewards as well. Family get the same kind of bonuses as everyone else. And as we'll see in the next chapter, they should be expected to work their way up the company ladder the same way any potential leader would.

Checking relationships also means family arguments that are fine at the dinner table stay at the dinner table. At home, your brother can be upset about how you got the better toys as kids. Your daughter can be angry at how you missed your grandchild's school performance. Your spouse can chew you out for failing to pick up the groceries on Saturday. In the office, though, everyone has to be a professional.

Once any member of the family walks across the threshold of the business, your relationship is a business one. This mindset is so central, all the rest of the tenets flow directly from it.

KEY #2: CREATE CLEAR ROLES AND RESPONSIBILITIES

In Chapter 6 we broke down the various functions within your company as well as the ways to measure each employee's success within that position. Those ideas aren't just useful for your standard employees; they are there for family as well.

In a family business, it's easy for responsibilities to drift across functions. Sometimes, in a small organization, that's inevitable, but no matter the size of your operation, your aim should be to codify clear divisions of responsibility for everyone.

That protects your family from being required to do more than you'd ask of any other employee, while protecting your company from family throwing their weight around and taking advantage of their privileged position. It also protects the company from family who feel they can take it easy because they have a personal relationship with the owner. If your cousin runs payroll, she should know the limits of that role. She should also know what that role entails, what you expect, what the pay is, and so on. She should know that she can't go and burst into a marketing meeting just because she's family with the boss. And she should know you won't ask her to run that meeting because you're short-staffed for the day.

In the office, she has a clear role, and she needs to fulfill it—just like everyone else.

KEY #3: TREAT EVERYONE THE SAME

Consequences are important in life. They reinforce the rules we're supposed to live by. We recognize that in our role as a parent. But we have to embrace that fact as a founder in our family business as well. If you'd fire someone else for a particular transgression, you have to be willing to do the same with family. And they need to know it.

If Tyler had been held accountable for taking other people's sales—the same way anyone else would have been—he would have either improved his behavior or gone out on his own to find a new career. If Carol told Jack he'd be fired for taking that vacation the same way any other employee would be, he'd know he couldn't take his job for granted.

Real consequences have to be in place if you want family to take the work seriously. Consequences are the bite you add to the other three keys. They force everyone to recognize that in the office they have to fulfill their roles, live those values, and behave like professionals. If they aren't willing to do so, they can find another job elsewhere.

Essentially, this is the enforcement mechanism that forces everyone to realize you will not play favorites. As a member of your family, you may feel they're entitled to a job in the company, but once they take that job, that's when the entitlement ends.

KEY #4: ESTABLISH CLEAR AND COMMITTABLE VALUES AND BEHAVIORS FOR ALL

We've already discussed your core values. Now it's time to live those values. When setting your core values, you should ask yourself a few key questions: Are you willing to fire an offender who breaks this value? Will you take a financial hit for it? Is it alive and well in your organization?

Before you nod your head in agreement to all those questions, consider who you're hypothetically holding accountable in your mind. For these values to really be part of your core, you have to be willing to hold family to those standards just as much as any other person in the company.

If that's the case, you have to make sure everyone—including family—understands those values and lives by them in the office. You may allow your kids or your uncle more leniency in your private life, but in the office, they have to behave the way you expect of every other employee.

KEY #5: ESTABLISH CLEAR COMMUNICATION

To ensure that your family have taken all of this on board, you have to establish clear communication. Communication is one of the biggest issues I hear about from the businesses I work with. Somewhere along the way, the intention of the founder is lost or the concerns of family become garbled. You may have a clear role in mind for your son or daughter, but if you can't communicate it to them clearly, that clarity doesn't matter—because the person who needs to know doesn't understand.

It doesn't have to be this way. We'll break down how you can communicate more clearly in Chapter 11. For now, the point is simply to recognize how central this key is to success in family business. Be intentional about what, when, and how things get communicated in your company, and many of the issues you see can be resolved before they ever cause a problem.

A PATH TO SUCCESS

These five keys lead to an obvious dilemma. We all know that family—at least certain family members—are not like every other employee. You intend to eventually put your son or daughter in a position of leadership, possibly with an aim of someday handing over the whole company to them.

That's a fine ambition, but as with everything else, there's a way you can go about this that allows your family members to feel they've earned a top role in your organization—while also allowing them to develop the skills, experience, and discipline to be a great leader. And that way forward is the development plan.

CHAPTER 9

FOLLOWING A DEVELOPMENT PLAN

THERE'S A FAMILY FARM IN THIS AREA. ONE OF THEIR MAIN products is sustainably grown cotton. It's guaranteed to be less harmful to the environment. It's becoming very popular across the whole country. For a while, Patricia, the founder of the family business, trusted one of her cousins to run the harvesting side of the business. He did well in the job, but he got restless and moved his family to Austin. Once they were settled, he didn't want to commute and left the company.

That left a leadership spot wide open. Patricia had a few experienced members of her team who could fill that spot. Instead, she chose Aaron, another cousin, to step in and run it.

Aaron definitely had a lot of potential. He was young, eager, and well-educated. He came in with a lot of energy, but unfortunately, Patricia had set him up to fail. Despite walking into leadership of a whole farm, he didn't know anything about cotton or harvesting it. On top of that, he was dealing with an alienated team that felt their people had been passed over. Some of the farm's top people began openly talking about finding work with a company where they could actually move up and advance their careers.

Aaron didn't have the knowledge of the industry or the experience in leadership to assuage the distrust he received from the team. Facing a huge loss in profits and team members, in short order, Patricia had to remove him from the position altogether.

THE RISK OF THROWING FAMILY INTO THE DEEP END

In Chapter 6, I briefly touched on the need to create a development plan for the family you hope to raise up to leadership. Creating a clear path to leadership is a crucial part of any people system, but it has particular relevance for family businesses. The reason for this is simple: far too many founders simply throw a family member into leadership just because they're family. And that can be incredibly disruptive.

In the first place, you can end up with the same kind of entitlement issues we've seen throughout this book. If family members know they're guaranteed a top position, they often enter the company feeling entitled to more pay and power without earning it. Why should they put in a full shift? Why should they bother learning how to do the job to the best of their abilities? The position is guaranteed.

That wasn't the case at Patricia's farm. Aaron was eager to work, but she did step into the second liability of running a business without a development plan. She risked losing all her best talent because they knew they'd never get to be leaders in her organization. It's hard to run a successful business if you lose all your A-players to your rivals. But that's the dynamic you can create if top positions are reserved solely for family—especially if those family members haven't proven they deserve them.

Even if you can avoid entitlement and all your A-players remain loyal, you still face some serious risks by throwing family straight into leadership. Without building a structure to raise family up through the business, you can install someone in a position of real consequence who doesn't understand the company, the product, the culture, or the customer. In other words, just like Patricia, you're setting them up to fail.

A PATH TO FAMILY LEADERSHIP

To avoid these risks, you need a development plan that allows family (or any other potential leaders in the organization, for that matter) to grow into their future leadership position. A development plan starts with finding a role where each family member can be successful with their current level of knowledge and skill. That first role should give them the opportunity to get their bearings and absorb the company culture and values. From there, you want to create a clear path they can move up in a logical way that allows them to earn their eventual high place in the company.

Ideally, you want to move them around the various corners of the business so they understand all the functions as well as you do, while slowly raising them up the ranks. If you run an auto repair shop, your kid might start running the register. They could later work on various types of repairs before moving to inventory and ordering parts. With each role, they might have a few more people under them. This would allow them to organically absorb all the knowledge they need and slowly adjust to leadership.

A good development plan allows family to learn everything they need to know, feel a sense of ownership over the company, and earn the respect of their fellow workers.

I saw the power of such a plan in real time at Interstate Batteries. Norm Miller had his son Scott work what was effectively a ten-year apprenticeship across every area of the business. Scott drove routes. He worked in accounting. He worked in advertising. He was in the warehouse and in stores. I'm sure Norm paid him well, but he made sure Scott knew everything about the business. He also made sure Scott respected all the various functions of the company and knew the people who would work under him.

Norm stuck to this plan even when he left. At that time, Scott still wasn't ready to take over. So they brought in a new CEO. It was only when that CEO left that Scott took over—finally fully ready to take complete control of things.

Interstate Batteries' story is amazing, but it isn't unique. I've seen similar success at multiple companies. For instance, there's a construction material supplier in our area. The founder successfully handed that company off to the second generation. Right now, they're working on generation number three. One of the current CEO's sons is already running operations and preparing to take over. His brother is now working at the counter for inside sales and doing distribution and routing for trucks—all while he's still in high school.

That's the ideal you want to aim for.

ACCEPT REALITY

A development plan is not a guarantee that family will rise through the ranks. Some people simply aren't meant for leadership—and every good founder has to recognize that possibility. There's a brewery in this area run by a woman named Penny and her two sons. One of her sons is an aggressive, tough-minded businessperson who is currently in charge of managing front of house and overseeing finance. He's got "future CEO" written all over him. The other is more passive and detail oriented. Penny wisely put him in charge of operations.

But there's still a problem. The passive son doesn't really take ownership of the job. He does what he's told, but he doesn't lead anyone. He's not going to drive results. That's just who he is.

This is why it's so important to have your priorities right in family business. Family comes first, and that means accepting family for who they are. Some people are great leaders; others aren't. Some are creative thinkers; others aren't.

You want to place your family in positions where they can thrive. And you want them at the level of leadership where they can do their best work—for themselves and for the company. It's great to create a plan for their rise through the company, but if they don't have the right qualities, it's better to leave them where they can succeed and be happy than to force them to move into positions where they could struggle and hurt the company.

STICKING TO THE RULES

In the last chapter, we set out the five keys to bringing family into your business. Here, I want to reiterate the main lesson from those keys: you have to stick to the rules when family enters the business. And that includes developing the talent of your family. That means you can't reward them if they don't earn it, and you can't avoid corrective action if they deserve it.

Everyone with a job in your company should know their role, their responsibilities, the potential incentives for doing well, and the potential consequences for falling short. Just because you want your son to take over in two years doesn't mean you should promote him to keep him on schedule if he hasn't earned it.

As with Interstate Batteries, sometimes it's better to bring in another leader and give family the time to rise naturally than to force it.

BE THE LEADER YOUR COMPANY NEEDS

To put a development plan in place requires vision, humility, and the proper use of authority. In other words, it requires leadership.

It can sometimes get lost in all the complexity of family and business that leadership is one of your main roles as a founder. You are meant to lead your family and the team in your business. Some of that may come intuitively. But there are few areas where a little improvement can make a bigger difference across all the important aspects of your life.

CHAPTER 10

LEADERSHIP

IN CHAPTER 8, I INTRODUCED CAROL AND DAVE, THE FOUNDers of a successful interior design business that now brings in $16 million in revenue each year. They've worked hard to achieve that level of success, and they're ready to mostly hand responsibility over to their sons, Bill and Jack. In her dreams, Carol would like to be able to step back from the business side entirely and focus on her real passion: designing her dream home for her retirement. Dave is ready to outright retire. But their sons simply aren't ready for leadership.

I've already described how Jack tried to take a vacation during the most important trade show of the year. But the problems go deeper than that. Bill is in charge of marketing and sales. He's got the skills to run the business, but he really doesn't know how to be a leader.

This became painfully apparent recently during our annual planning session. We sat down together for nine hours of planning—but we spent seven of those hours arguing. And the main culprit for the arguments was Bill.

He started chucking rocks at his brother for his lack of direction and at his parents for failing to complete certain tasks they were still responsible for. That put everyone on the defensive and turned our conversation into one of constant recriminations.

By the end of our time, Dave walked out saying, "I'm tired of coming to these meetings."

Bill wasn't completely wrong to be upset with people. Jack really wasn't pulling his weight yet. Dave was mostly checked out and hadn't helped make this a smooth transfer of power. And Carol was so busy trying to do everything, she wasn't helping bring others into the company to fill the gaps she'd leave behind.

When tempers cooled, I told him that, but I also told him that the biggest problem his family and business faced was coming from him. His leadership style was making everything worse. He was focused on having power, where he needed to be focused on having authority. He was supposed to be the new founder, but he wasn't acting like one.

"Leadership isn't just about having the power in your company," I told him, "it's about becoming the leader your company needs."

COACHING MAKES THE DIFFERENCE

Some time ago, I was at a party where I met Timmy Newsome, a former running back for the Dallas Cowboys. We got to talking about the game, and he told me something extremely interesting about leadership.

Timmy said that at the NFL level, there was very little difference between the quality of players on each team. Almost everyone in the locker room had been the best player on their college team. Most of them had been All-Americans.

"The difference between a winning team and a losing team is not talent at that level," he told me. "It's coaching."

This is why we celebrate great coaches even though they aren't on the field when their teams win. Great coaches—like my personal favorite, Cowboys coach Tom Landry—know how to lead their teams. They know when to be hard on them and when to go easier. They know how to build support and push them to their peak performance. They can communicate. They can inspire. And that leads to some incredible results on the field.

In fact, it can do even more than that. After Coach Landry passed away, many former players talked about the impact he had on their lives. He influenced way more than just their performances on the field. He helped shape them into good people.

That's what great leadership looks like. It's what great leadership can do for your company. But it's only possible if you are able to grow into a leader who can help your people reach that level.

WHAT DID I DO?

If you want to improve as a leader, you have to start by accepting the responsibility of leadership. And that means looking at yourself before blaming others. What did you do that created the difficult scenario you're facing? What can you do next time to make sure it doesn't happen again?

You have to commit to improving. That's the only way forward.

If a project ended up delayed, was it the laziness of your team or was there miscommunication coming from the top? If sales are down, is that due to workers who don't care about their job or have you struggled to inspire them and model your expectations? Whether it's a process problem or a people problem, it's definitely a leadership problem.

This isn't an opinion. It's been proven. In the book *Extreme*

Ownership, authors Jocko Willink and Leif Babin shared some of the lessons they learned as Navy SEALs. One of those lessons involved a raft race. The SEALs had a competition in which six teams would get into rubber rafts, paddle out into the ocean, go around a buoy, and then come back. Every time they had the race, the same team won and the same team finished sixth.

It would be easy to assume that the team coming in sixth simply wasn't good enough, but SEALs don't do anything easy. So they tried an experiment. They took the leader from the winning raft and switched him with the leader of the team coming in sixth. The result? The first-place team once again finished first—but the other team went from sixth to second.

It wasn't the team that was holding that raft back, it was the leader. Everything in the organization rises and falls with leadership. If there are problems, it's up to the leader to find solutions.

Sometimes, the changes required are far less radical than you expect. I've seen plenty of situations cleared up by leadership sending emails after an important conversation to remind everyone of their new responsibilities. Other times, a change in how meetings are run allows for better ideas to develop across the whole team.

Essentially, before you start chucking rocks at anyone else, be sure you're not living in a glass house.

That's not to say you're always at fault. Some workers are lazy. Some people don't care about their jobs. But a leader always starts with themself and asks how well they're leading. They hold themself accountable. Only then do they look elsewhere.

ADJUSTING YOUR LEADERSHIP STYLE

One of the most impactful ways you can improve as a leader is to really consider your leadership style. Some people are born with innate leadership skills that inspire their people and create strong teams that are always overperforming. But most of us have to work on this. We have to examine how we interact with our people.

Leaders come in three general styles: diminishers, neutralizers, and enhancers.

Diminishers are all about themselves. They love to compare their efforts to others—with others always looking worse. Every conversation seems to point to how much harder they work than anyone else. Unfortunately, this motivation tends to result in those leaders taking credit for other people's work. Accomplishments belong to them; failures belong to others. Diminishers are negative, condescending, and critical. And basically, people don't like working for them.

This is the problem Bill has. He may not mean to diminish the efforts of others or take credit for their contribution, but that is how he comes across to others in the business. In that planning meeting, for instance, Bill minimized or ignored all the hard work everyone else in the family had done in order to focus solely on where they were deficient. He refused to give anyone credit for their successes and instead focused on all the extra time he was putting in.

He needs to change that—because diminishers often struggle to hold onto their best people. And when it comes to family, diminishers struggle to maintain good relationships with family who get into business with them.

I've seen the impact of working for a diminisher firsthand. I was one of those people who walked away, even though I had a clear career path ahead of me. Right out of college, I was recruited by JCPenney. I liked the work, but my boss was a real diminisher. Despite working hard and doing well, nothing was ever good enough. At my first review, I was dinged for fixing a problem but not doing it exactly to the specifications my boss set.

That was the beginning of the end for me. From then on, I was "quiet quitting," doing the bare minimum until I could find something better. When I resigned, the manager above my boss called me into his office. He couldn't believe I was leaving.

"Give me a different team and a different boss," I told him, "and I'll stay." They couldn't do it, so I left. I've been a major asset to other companies. I've built my own businesses. I could have turned all that energy toward JCPenney, but one diminisher convinced me to go elsewhere.

Compared to diminishers, neutralizers are better—but they are still limited leaders. Neutralizers are defined by their passivity. They work hard, but they focus on their role and not enough on everyone else. When they're in charge of a project or an account, everything gets done because they'll do all the work themselves. As soon as they turn their attention elsewhere, everything falls apart.

This is the type of leadership Jack and his father, Dave, offered. They would do the work required, but they had no talent to inspire or hold others accountable. If there were problems beyond the work itself—arguments between team members, outside concerns—they walked away. As Dave became more disengaged from his own responsibilities, his own productivity declined, without anyone on his team capable of picking up the slack.

This is why in leadership you have to aim to become an enhancer. Enhancers—or as Liz Wiseman calls them, multipliers—want to get the best out of everybody. Their agenda is not the priority. They check their personal interests at the door because they want to get the best out of everyone. They want to encourage, promote, drive home values, and help people work together.

In the interior design business, the only person trying to be an enhancer was Carol. It's no coincidence that the business began to see such fractures when she started trying to step away. No one else was seeking to enhance everyone in the company.

USING YOUR TIME WELL

Style is important, but it isn't everything. Stepping into leadership requires you to develop a whole new set of skills. This is why family businesses so often bang their heads up against the Peter Principle. A family member who was a great salesperson may not make a great leader of that same department.

This is a particular risk for family businesses because these companies often lack the training and coaching to help prepare people for their new roles. In a Fortune 500 company, moving into the C-suite will include instruction on how your role has changed. You'll have multiple examples around you that show how you should now conduct yourself. The CEO succession process almost always includes several months of coaching about the new role. None of that exists in most family businesses.

The skills required in leadership is such a vast topic, we can only scratch the surface here, but we can begin with how you use your time. Often, moving up in an organization means taking on ever more important or complex work in your particular function—ever bigger clients, ever more complex HR concerns, etc.—until it doesn't. Once you reach the leadership level, those basic business tasks are no longer your responsibility. You delegate them. You don't fix the problems, you get people on your team who can fix those problems on their own. And if they can't fix them, you get new people who can.

Instead of putting all your time into these core tasks, leaders should split their time into thirds. One third should be spent building and developing their team. Another third should be spent on strategy and planning. And the last third should be their work responsibilities. Typically, though, without training and discipline, the last third eats the first two.

That does no one any good. It forces leaders into being neutralizers, doing all the work and none of the leadership. And when no time is spent on teams or strategy, there's no direction or improvement in performance. This is another issue that the interior design business is facing. Because everyone spends their time doing those standard work tasks, they never train anyone up to handle those tasks for them. For that reason, everyone in the family is chronically overworked and has no time to improve things. No wonder they end up at each other's throats.

If you can change these dynamics in your company and divide your time better, production and profits can skyrocket. This creates a virtuous cycle. If you spend time building your team, their performance improves, and you don't need to supervise so much. That frees up more time to strategize, further improving results.

But this kind of leadership requires a shift in mindset. One of the reasons leaders spend all their time on the day-to-day standard tasks is because it feels good to complete projects. Many leaders struggle to feel they've accomplished anything when they didn't directly do the work. But for a leader, a good day isn't spent doing the work; it's spent ensuring the work is done right by those below them.

If you can absorb that idea, you can begin to adjust your time to match what is actually needed of you.

SHARE YOUR KNOWLEDGE

The more you improve as a leader, the more you should share the tools and insights that helped you get there. You aren't the only leader in your organization. Often, your family members in the business are feeling the same way you do. They are resentful because they feel they do all the work and their teams don't do anything. They're burned-out neutralizers who have no idea that things can work more effectively.

Helping them helps the business. It will improve performance at every level. At the same time, it prepares family to someday take over. If you don't equip your family with leadership skills now, you're once again setting them up to fail. They'll simply move up and continue doing what doesn't work.

There's a reason rookies rarely start in the NFL. Unless they're truly a generational talent, they usually spend that first season training, developing new mindsets, and gaining understanding of new processes. They ride the bench and make brief appearances. Teams invest so much in them with so little early output because the game is played on a level they have never experienced before. Just throwing them in is a recipe for disaster.

It's the same with leadership. Don't just promote your kid and hope they can figure out how to lead their team. Train them, give them a chance to shadow you, get them some coaching. Do the prep work so they can succeed.

And encourage them to share their own insights. One of the best succession stories I've ever seen involved a son who went off and got an MBA. He learned all kinds of new leadership skills. Instead of keeping them to himself, the founder of the family business encouraged him to share what he'd learned. Thanks to him, everyone was able to use those new ideas, so all the leaders could develop. When he eventually took over, everyone knew he was prepared.

Of course, for this sharing to occur, there has to be strong communication skills across the family and the business. And that requires another entirely new set of skills.

CHAPTER 11

COMMUNICATION

IT'S BEEN A WHILE SINCE WE CHECKED IN ON PETER AND HIS family business. If you remember, he ran a multifaceted business with a plumbing company and a number of franchise stores. There were many family business problems keeping him from peace at home and prosperity in the office. He didn't have the control of his finances he needed to *explain* why he made certain decisions that upset his children. He lacked the strategy he could *share* with his family that would make clear where the company was going. And he didn't *lay out* clear roles and responsibilities for all of his kids.

But within both of those problems, you can find one particularly significant issue that was creating much of the tension Peter was facing: poor communication.

We could start with the poor communication with his daughter, Jessica, about her responsibilities when she ran plumbing, as well as the poor communication around the equity he had promised her. Or we could look at his poor communication with Zach, the middle son, who never had very clear responsibilities or authority. This allowed him to be idle and unproductive while still pulling in a huge paycheck.

Or we could consider his poor communication with Eric, his oldest, who thought he had the right to fire Zach for his poor performance. And then there's Sam, the baby of the family, who never got clear communication about why his profits were going to other companies.

As I said, there were many issues here for Peter to untangle, but the one problem that ran through everything else was poor communication. He had never sat his children down and explained things clearly. And that came back to haunt him over and over again.

THE RISK OF POOR COMMUNICATION

Whenever I survey a dysfunctional team, the number one problem is always poor communication. When I ask around, the most common response I hear from people is, "I don't know what's going on."

Communication really is a critical leadership skill in a business. It determines your level of influence. You can't get people to perform if you can't communicate what you need them to do. No one can follow your strategy or fulfill a role if they don't understand what you're asking of them.

Just as good communication can give people clarity, poor communication can lead to a multitude of problems through misunderstanding. When communication is poor, gossip fills in many of the gaps. Over time, a team can come to live in a "spirit of fear, " filling those gaps not just with gossip but with negative assumptions about the health of the organization and the security of their own jobs.

Employees hearing a company is being acquired may assume they'll lose their job. A VP of sales, hearing the company is struggling for profitability, may assume they aren't getting a bonus despite putting up great numbers. And these workers may respond by looking for work elsewhere—even if their job or their bonus is secure.

If that isn't clearly communicated, the company may lose their best people for no reason.

And that's not just the case with your employees. It's true of family as well. If you don't communicate all the ideas we've covered in this book to every family member in the business, those ideas are essentially worthless. If you can't communicate it, it's like those changes don't exist at all.

TWO-WAY COMMUNICATION

Communication is the first skill we learn as children. When we're hungry or have a wet diaper, we cry. Unfortunately, many of us never advance beyond this basic level of communication. We remain focused on our own needs and cry out whenever we feel those needs aren't being met. You only need to look at some of the dysfunctional family business offices I visit to see how common this primitive form of communication is.

The arguments between Eric, Zach, and Sam definitely have an air of "crying as communication." Everyone complains all the time, and everyone is looking out solely for themselves and what they feel belongs to them. Whether it's income, investible profits, or power, none of Peter's children are looking to understand one another or compromise. They want to cry until the founder fixes things.

To move beyond crying, we have to change how we communicate—and that starts with moving from one-way communication to two-way communication. This is difficult for people in the modern world because so much of our communication is one-way these days. We send emails and texts. At most, we might leave a voicemail. In one-way communication, we have no idea if the person on the other side really understands us. We have to assume they interpreted the message correctly.

But we all know that often isn't the case. I recently got an email from a client. In it, she wrote about how she felt we weren't making enough progress. She felt her company needed something new. I wrote her back and said that I understood. We could end our business relationship, so she could find a new coach. But that wasn't what she meant at all. She wanted me to bring some new tools and suggestions to our next meeting. She assumed that message was clear from her email, but it wasn't as far as I was concerned.

This same limitation can creep into in-person conversation. This is how Peter and Eric ended up with opposite interpretations for dealing with Zach. Peter thought he'd made clear that Zach's job was secure, while Eric felt he had permission to fire his brother. While they were standing right next to each other, neither one truly understood the other.

To create more two-way conversation opportunities, there are a couple major changes you can institute. First, put more effort into in-person communication. While this clearly isn't a guarantee of understanding, it does make understanding more likely. You need people in the same place (or very least seeing each other on a screen) to create the opportunity for more communication clarity.

With people together, you can then follow Stephen R. Covey's advice in *The 7 Habits of Highly Effective People* and seek first to understand and only then to be understood. You can't communicate well if you don't understand the other person in the conversation. And you increase that understanding by exercising one of the fundamental leadership skills: learning to ask questions. To borrow the title from John Maxwell's excellent book: good leaders ask great questions.

A great question elicits the other person's genuine thoughts and their feedback. It also allows you to determine whether the other person has a clear understanding of the points under discussion. If Peter had done this, he not only would have understood Eric's concerns more deeply, he could have ensured Eric understood the limits of his authority.

This isn't an easy skill to master—it does take work. But with time, you can improve two-way communication with everyone in your family business. And that can lead to mutual listening and understanding that reduces the space for misinterpretation.

TONE IT DOWN

To improve your listening skills, you have to summon a quality many of us are in short supply of: humility. Instead of expecting everyone to do the work to understand you, take a step back and ask whether you are doing enough to ensure they understand things as you intended. In particular, ask yourself whether you're using the right tone to help your people reach the understanding you want them to have.

This takes constant mindfulness. Far too often, I see founders who have a habit of blowing off steam and saying things they don't really mean in a tone that suggests they really do. After losing a customer, they may shout that the company is going bankrupt. A costly delay leads them to insist that everyone in the office deserves to get fired. After an exhausting week, they say they'd sell the company immediately if only a buyer would come in.

Most of the time, they don't mean any of this, but say something loudly and often enough and people think it's true. A company I work with lost their best employee because the owners kept talking about being out of cash. They weren't actually out of cash. In fact, they were doing quite well. They just had a couple tight months while they waited for some invoices to get paid. But this employee took them at their word and left.

You have to be mindful of the tone of your conversation. Do you always sound angry? Do you always voice negative thoughts? Do you rely on threats that you don't follow through on? Do you fail to leave room for positive comments and reinforcement?

These patterns can create a toxic environment in which communication is not only poor but in which no one really wants to communicate anyway.

WATCH YOUR BODY LANGUAGE

Up to this point, we've discussed the importance of improving listening, language, and tone in our communication, but these actually make up only a fraction of the information that really allows people to understand what we mean. Seventy percent of our communication is actually based on body language. It's how we look more than what we say.

I was sitting in on a family business conversation recently in which the son who was being groomed to take over the business really went after his parents, the founders who had built the business from scratch. It wasn't the words or the tone that really upset his parents, though. It was his body language. The way he stood, the positioning of his hands, the look in his eyes, it all came across as aggressive, annoyed, and frustrated. When the parents tried to explain themselves, his body language was dismissive.

Even if he'd said all the right words, he would have done real damage to that relationship.

When I got hold of him, he confessed that he had been upset—but not about the business. He was getting married soon, and his mom was struggling to handle both her wedding obligations and her responsibilities within the business. He perceived her delays as a personal attack. That fed into the body language he displayed when discussing business issues in that meeting. He had meant to communicate some professional difficulties. Instead, all he communicated was how angry he was.

To avoid this, we have to be more aware of body language—and not just what our bodies are communicating but what others are as well. Experts say 70 percent of communication comes through body language, so it matters how you present yourself while you deliver a message. As you speak, look at the body language of those you're communicating with. Do they look enthusiastic or uncomfortable? Are they nodding along, showing their understanding, or do they seem perplexed?

If you watch their body language, it will tell you when misunderstanding is occurring even without anyone saying a word.

FOLLOW UP ON YOUR COMMUNICATION

These communication tools are valuable for every aspect of your life, but as a founder running a family business, they matter most when you are trying to get people to complete the tasks you need them to complete.

Part of your job is to hold people accountable, but you can only do that if you create the communication structures that eliminate excuses and misunderstanding.

Accountability is powerful. I once lost a client precisely because they felt I wasn't holding them accountable enough. When they told me they were going elsewhere, I pointed out that I'd advised them on the steps they had to take. I couldn't hire more people for them or expand their products into a new market. I couldn't reorganize their operations. They had to do that for themselves.

But they felt I hadn't done enough to follow up and keep them on task. My occasional emails weren't enough.

I learned an important lesson that day. These days, I always follow up regularly and check if agenda items are completed. I'm sure the frequency of my messages annoys some clients, but it remains a very popular strategy with most of them.

You have to do the same with your team. Within a conversation, review the deliverables directly. "When did I say that was due?" People work better with deadlines, so set them and make sure they're understood. Ask for questions and seek out any misunderstanding in the moment. Then, you can follow up with those one-way communicators. Send an email or a text to remind them and put the assignment in writing.

It's easy for a founder to assume family understands them. After all, they know you as well as anyone. But family as much as anyone else needs clear instructions and follow-ups to keep them on track. After all, in the office, they should be treated just like any other employee.

SETTING TIME ASIDE FOR COMMUNICATION

One of the reasons Peter struggled so much to communicate with his children is that he rarely had them all together. There were so many petty disagreements between them that they never wanted to sit down and hash out their problems or find solutions.

As adults, that was their prerogative in their personal lives. But as the founder of the family business, Peter had the ability to do something about it in the office. He might not want to make them work closely day to day, but there was an opportunity to get everyone together to make sure everyone understood one another and their own responsibilities: the family council.

CHAPTER 12

CREATE A FAMILY COUNCIL

WITH HIS SONS READY TO TEAR EACH OTHER APART, PETER came to me in desperation. Despite all his best efforts, he couldn't seem to get Eric, Zach, and Sam to agree or even to sit down and talk to each other. How could he get everyone on the same page if they wouldn't listen?

This had been a problem for a while, but it suddenly became a crisis when Zach came to him with a plan he wanted Peter to finance. His idea was to leave the family business and build his own company by investing in three areas: a cabinet shop, an RV park, and a new storage unit complex. To do all this, he'd need a million-dollar loan.

Peter was a bit flummoxed. He told Zach he couldn't just give him the million dollars with no strings. Instead, he'd loan it only if he received 60 percent of the equity in these new businesses. Once Zach paid back the loan, he could own the business outright.

Zach did not take the offer well. Nor did his brothers like the idea that he was asking for a lot of money behind their backs. If you recall, Sam, the youngest, had been complaining that the profits from the plumbing business he ran were being invested elsewhere in the family business. Why did Zach deserve a million dollars for leaving when Sam (and Eric) were working so hard to build value within the company?

The situation seemed certain to spiral out of control.

To avoid a falling-out with all his sons and potentially harming the business at the same time, I suggested Peter consider a novel solution: a family business council. This would be an opportunity for everyone to come together in one room and talk through the major issues affecting the business. How should they structure equity? What was the exit strategy if one of the kids wanted to leave the business? If they exited, could they come back? Who was going to take over the entire business someday? What responsibilities should each person in the family hold?

With a family business council in place, everyone would have a voice. Everyone would have a chance to participate. And just maybe, everyone could come to a resolution they could live with on these big controversies.

REDUCE FRICTION IN DECISIONS

Family business is often derailed by miscommunication and accusations of favoritism. Peter's daughter, Jessica, felt she and her husband weren't being treated as well as her brothers, so she left. Zach felt the same way. So did Sam and Eric. Somehow, the only thing every child could agree on was that they were the one being treated less fairly than all the others.

The best way to reduce these accusations is through better communication that includes more transparency and communal decisions. That's what a family council can offer. It forces everyone to sit in the same room and hear each other out. Because everyone has to decide what changes they really want to see, fight for them, and judge other options, it makes everyone think more deeply about those decisions.

It also allows family members who don't get along to limit their interactions to just the council. Since things were tense between all the brothers, they had fallen into the habit of bringing all requests and complaints straight to Mom or Dad. A family council created a forum where they would only have to be in the room together for one hour a week, at which point they could hear each other out and then ignore one another for another seven days.

This forum created the space for communication and problem-solving, which are key to maintaining buy-in in the family and the business. It's an environment where everybody can feel they win, and everybody recognizes they are winning.

MORE CLARITY, LESS DRAMA

The family council has the unique ability to bring otherwise unspoken issues to a head. If you can get all your family in a room with the express purpose of airing the most important issues in the business, a lot of truth can come out.

In the family council for the interior design business, for instance, the father, Dave, outright told the rest of his family, "I don't want to be here anymore." The venue allowed him to share his feelings that he was ready to retire and he was tired of family drama in the business. Instead of everyone guessing and putting their own reasons behind his behavior, everyone was finally on the same page. And that is very valuable.

Everyone benefits when they know where they stand. In Peter's case, part of the issue with Zach was that he hadn't actually detailed why he couldn't just hand his son a check for a million dollars. Like many founders, he'd done his best to shelter his children from all the tough choices he'd had to make to create the success they enjoyed. But at a certain point, that actually does more harm than good. They needed to know the reasoning behind his decisions.

There are consequences for every decision and behavior: consequences for disrespect, poor investment, or questionable management. But Peter's children had never truly seen the downside of running a business or the sacrifices required to make it a success. And Peter found it difficult to change that dynamic in normal conversations. The kids would roll their eyes or feel like he was making excuses.

That's what he could offer in the family council. It offered him a neutral location to talk through why the kids couldn't have everything they wanted—at least not all at once. He could explain why, despite the company doing so well, it was difficult to write a million-dollar check without any equity or certainty of repayment.

This was also the perfect opportunity for him to get truly honest about what he wanted from the business. Peter had always had a vision of his business being a way to keep the kids together and make sure everyone had enough and got along. But because he had never truly communicated that, they had to interpret his decisions on their own. They painted the picture with their own perception. Peter could correct that in the family council.

Finally, the family council also gave Peter the space for intervention. It was a place to lay out the destructive behavior he'd seen in his kids and make clear that such behavior would no longer be tolerated. Sam's constant questioning, Eric overstepping, Zach underperforming—it all had to end. But it was easier to ensure it would end in a family council conversation where everyone could voice their feelings and hear one another out.

COUNCIL RULES

The family council obviously offers a lot of potential benefits—but only if you run it properly. Some aspects of your council will be distinctive. Every family council should follow the unique needs of the family and business at the center of it. You may need multiple meetings a week or only one a month. You might want to set special rules about what can be introduced or what topics won't be discussed. You might invite certain family members to join who aren't in the business but play a founder role in the family. And so on.

All that being said, there are some basic rules all family councils should follow.

First, **meetings should be scheduled regularly**. Again, the frequency is up to you, but everyone should know when the next council is taking place. That regularity allows you to deal with normal business and not just meet in crisis when everyone is already upset. The council becomes another part of business as usual.

You also want **attendance to be mandatory**. Obviously, people get sick, there are business trips that can't be canceled, and other reasonable excuses. But as much as possible, everyone should be expected to attend. The council only works if everyone sits down together.

And since everyone is coming, make sure they all have a role to play. There should always be **a clear agenda** to follow and responsibilities for each member of the family in that agenda. You should publish the agenda and roles prior to the meeting so everyone can prepare. This also signals that this isn't a family catch-up session or an opportunity to hash out old arguments from childhood. This is a business meeting. If there's no agenda, there's no meeting.

Since this is a business meeting, the aim has to be to come to some resolution on the issues that are raised. And that requires **a decision-making process**. How should your family decide on a direction for each topic under discussion? Does everyone have to agree? Do you need a simple majority? Is it two-thirds to win the day? Whatever your decision here, make it clear to everyone what is required to change rules or strategy. Also, there should always be a veto vote for the founder here. If all the kids decide to gang up and vote for Mom or Dad to write them million-dollar checks, the founder has to be able to say no. Ultimately, this is your company, and you have to reserve the right to make the big decisions and make them your way.

Finally, to help keep the temperature low and get through the agenda, you need **a neutral third party** to facilitate the meeting. This third party should not be family or work directly in the business. It should be clear to everyone that this third party consultant doesn't have anything to gain other than to help the family get more peace and prosperity. This allows them to help develop the agenda, put items up for vote, document decisions, and crucially, step in as referee when needed without accusations of bias.

Without a third-party facilitator, the founder is likely to step in and run the council. But that can lead back to the same kinds of misunderstandings we're trying to avoid. If the founder is the one who decides to move on from an item or who tells one sibling to hear another out, that can come across as favoritism. If it's a neutral party, though, they can get people to listen and move forward without dredging up all those unhelpful familial accusations.

PREPARING TO STEP AWAY

A family council isn't a perfect solution to everything. Peter's family is still struggling with their issues and with the council itself. Eric always shows up, but Sam has missed a few councils, and Zach only ever came to one. They still haven't perfected a way to reach big decisions as a family.

Luckily, though, they have time to work this out. Peter is still relatively young and engaged in the business. He has time on his side to work out the kinks and get everyone on board.

Or at least, that's how it feels right now. But as I've told Peter before, that's no excuse to put off planning for a future in which there is no more time. Instead of assuming he has tomorrow and the next day and so on for years and years to come, it's better to work on making everything work now—and preparing everyone for the day they have to run the company on their own. Because none of us know how long we have. And a clear succession plan is one of the greatest gifts we can leave our family.

CHAPTER 13

PREPARE FOR SUCCESSION

WHEN CALVIN TOOK OVER HIS FAMILY MOTORCYCLE BUSINESS a few years back, the succession plan went just as predicted. He knew the business top to bottom, and he stepped into leadership with enviable ease. It looked like the company was set for a long period of sustained success.

Then the worst tragedy that can befall a family occurred. Calvin was out riding his motorcycle one night when he got into an accident. He died from the injuries he sustained.

This would have been a horrible blow to the family on its own, but things were even worse than they at first appeared—because Calvin had left no succession plan in place. That meant not only that the family was grieving, but their business—their sole source of income—was also at risk.

The family had no idea who should take over. Who was going to call the shots? Who was in charge?

That's when his wife, Christina, stepped in. Calvin had willed her 20 percent of the company, and she wanted a seat at the table. In fact, she wanted more than a seat; she wanted to run the whole business. The family reluctantly agreed.

Christina was smart and motivated. She wanted to do well. The problem was that she didn't really know the business the way Calvin had. She often had to ask how things worked or why they worked that way. Understandably, she wanted to shake things up and busy herself restructuring the company. But with no experience in this area, she created more chaos than efficiency.

It's created a lot of disruption, which has drained the business of revenue when the family has needed it most.

YOU DON'T KNOW HOW LONG YOU HAVE

Calvin's story is truly tragic. In fact, it's so tragic, it's almost unthinkable for many of us. We don't want to imagine a world in which we die before we're ready, leaving our family and business in chaos. But none of us knows whether we'll get as much time as we planned for on this earth.

I'm no exception. Last autumn, I was doing fine, feeling pretty healthy. I was working hard and making plans for family and business for many years into the future. Suddenly, I developed a gallbladder issue that put me in intensive care for much of December. My life was never truly in danger, but it was a scary moment all the same.

In a way, I was lucky. I got another chance. Not everybody does. I helped a friend of mine, Joel Tardy, sell his family business a few years back. Selling allowed him to secure the future for his wife and twelve children. Joel had huge plans for his future. He moved to Nashville and became an incredible artist. You can see some of his work online today.

But Joel didn't know how little time he had left. A year after retiring, he died from pancreatic cancer. The only consolation was that he'd secured his family's financial position beforehand.

I bring up these examples because I know how hard it is to

face mortality. But as the founder of the family business, you have to have the courage to change what needs to be changed and to prepare for a future without you. And you have to do it **now**.

If you don't, you risk making your loss even more difficult for your family. Leaving the business behind without a succession plan can create massive potential for fighting among family members. If no one knows who should take over and no one is prepared to take over, everyone can start fighting for the top position while no one is actually ready for it.

That kind of chaos can destroy a business and a family.

This risk isn't just for family businesses. Deloitte has calculated that a failure to set up a succession plan costs American businesses $15 billion every year.

In other words, this is not optional. If you care about your family and your business, you have to create a succession plan—and you have to do it now.

CHOOSE WHAT'S BEST FOR ALL

When deciding what happens next for your business, you really have four options on the table:

- Sell it
- Bring in a manager while you and the family step back to enjoy the profits
- Hand the company down to one or more members of your family
- Shut it down

That's really all you can do.

Most of us want our business to continue beyond us. We want option three to work out. But that's also the most treacherous option. Ford is still a family company, but there have been periods when the family member in charge failed significantly. Henry Ford initially passed the company to his Edsel. When Edsel died from cancer in 1943, though, no one was prepared to take over. Henry had to step back in, even though he was no longer mentally and physically capable of running the company. It was only when Henry Ford II took over that they were able to steady things and lead the company forward.

There are plenty of examples of children inheriting a company only to run it into the ground. It happens every day in family business. The kids have the wrong temperament or lack the necessary skills. They don't want to do the work or prioritize taking out profits over growing the business.

Such succession failures can happen in a million ways. If you want to avoid that future, you have to be very careful in choosing this path and in choosing who you want to walk it with. It's crucial to identify the person in the family most capable and interested in taking over and to start developing them for their future role early.

As I've already related, the success of Interstate Batteries' succession comes down to Norm Miller's ability to recognize that his son, Scott, could be a great leader and his determination to make sure Scott was prepared for that future.

Ask yourself if the person you are considering has the competencies to really take the lead. Just because they're family doesn't mean they have the characteristics to be a founder. Do they have the drive, the grit, the creativity, the communication skills, and the financial savvy to take the company forward?

Importantly, this doesn't mean they have to be the same type of person as you. They may be quiet where you're loud, more extroverted where you're introverted. They might read more or less than you. They might have a higher or lower risk tolerance.

They could have different ambitions for the company than you. All of that is fine, so long as they have the key talents and the interest to lead.

These qualities are likely innate. They're either there or they aren't. All you can do is recognize them and help bring them out. I was once in a church service with the incredible Deion Sanders, and he said something that's always stuck with me. He told all of us, "If you're a jerk before you have money, all money does is make you more of a jerk. I know people with ten times the money I have who are the biggest jerks walking around."

The same is true of leaders. If you're a good leader before taking the top job, you'll likely be a good leader when you get it. If you're a bad leader before you're CEO, becoming CEO isn't going to change anything.

If the person you want to take over lacks those necessary leadership qualities, it's better to consider other options: either finding someone else to lead or considering a sale, a manager, or just shutting things down. You don't want to bet everything on the slim chance they become a completely different person when they take on the most important role of their lives.

CREATE A PATH TO A NEW OWNER

Eric, the oldest son of Peter, whom we've been following this whole book, recently told his father that he wants to buy him out. He was looking for a quick solution to all the family business problems. If Eric was in charge, there'd be no question about what to do with the second brother, Zach. And Eric believed he could come to an understanding with Sam more easily as well. The only hitch was that Eric wasn't in charge. Why not change that?

"Fine," Peter said, "but it's going to cost $100 million. That's how much I have wrapped up in this company. If you want it, you have to pay me a fair price."

Once again, as with so many of Peter's well-intentioned efforts, this did not go over well with his son. And for understandable reasons. That kind of money was impossible to raise. It was as close to a no as you could communicate with a dollar sign.

But it didn't have to be such a negative conversation. What Eric needs more than control right now is a clear path to someday taking over. This is what Norm at Interstate Batteries did so well. He laid out a development plan and a timeline for Scott that allowed him to learn every side of the business as he prepared to someday take over.

Peter could offer the same to Eric.

It's the same situation we've been dealing with in the interior design business as well. Dave, the father, has made it clear he wants out, but his wife, Carol, isn't quite ready to walk away. That's created an unbalanced company in which Carol and the oldest son, Bill, do almost everything, while the younger son, Jack, and Dave put in the minimal amount of effort required to keep the doors open.

To change that dynamic, they have laid out a roadmap that labels what everyone does right now and what everyone has to be doing when it's time for Mom and Dad to formally exit the company. Having laid out their start point and end point, they've begun charting a path to where everyone wants to arrive.

You can do this yourself pretty easily. List all the various functions in your company. Who is responsible for each right now? Now, let's do a mental exercise. If you weren't here tomorrow, who would take over each role?

You need a name to put for each function. That should be the person you intend to lead in that department at some point in the future.

Once you know that, you can begin to train everyone toward their future roles. If one of your children will someday take over finance, they can start learning everything about that role today. That way, no matter how long it is before they take over, they're ready.

At the same time, you can lay the legal and professional groundwork for them to take over. If they need to be on certain accounts to access the company's finances, get them the necessary permissions for that now. If they need to know all your VIP clients to someday take over sales, introduce them now. Create the framework for them to succeed whenever they're called upon to do so.

Hopefully, they get to step in according to your ideal timeline, but if it isn't ideal, they'll all be able to step in without any unnecessary chaos.

DON'T BECOME WED TO ONE EXIT

In the interior design business, Dave has been having a tough time. At a recent family council, Bill yelled at him for not fulfilling his responsibilities. It's true that Dave has been a bit checked out, but that was no excuse for his son's behavior. After the meeting, I asked if he would have accepted that kind of treatment from any other person in his company. The answer was an emphatic no.

"Then why do you take it from your son?"

Dave's reasoning for accepting such poor behavior was simple: Bill was the one they'd chosen to take over. If Dave put his foot down, that could blow up their entire exit strategy.

But there are times when it's best to reconsider your choices. It may be that Bill can improve his leadership and rise to the occasion, but Dave and Carol shouldn't assume that will happen. Again, as Deion Sanders suggested, most of the time, people don't change. And every founder has to be willing to adapt their plans to align with that reality.

Sometimes, the person you think has the right temperament turns out to show a different side of themself over time. The person you think has the right skills proves there are certain leadership qualities they'll never master.

It takes courage to be willing to recognize this. The fear that a change in plans can put your relationship at risk is real. For that reason, I'd say a change should be seen as a last resort, but you have to at least leave that door open.

Sometimes, the right change is simply to abandon a certain succession plan entirely. If your children seem unable to rise to the role of leadership in your company, it may be better to consider selling or handing the company off to a manager outside the family.

There's no shame in handing things off or even shutting your doors forever. Remember, family should come first. And if it's a choice between destroying relationships, setting your kids up to fail, and walking away from the business, that final option is likely the best one.

SHARE YOUR EXIT STRATEGY

Whatever your plan, make sure that everyone in the family business knows it as soon as possible. Communicate who will take over, when, how, and why. Whether you decide to share this in one-on-one meetings or lay it out at a family council meeting, you want to make sure everyone knows what's coming.

The value of this is that everyone knows what page they're on. Some of your kids may not like that their brother or sister is going to take over, but everyone will know what's expected of them and who will someday be in charge.

Once again, clarity is your ally. With a clear plan, everyone can effectively move toward their future roles, and you can prepare for the day you are going to step away—whether it's today or in twenty years.

CHAPTER 14

LEARN TO LEAVE WORK BEHIND

ONE OF THE REASONS DAVE AND CAROL'S INTERIOR DESIGN business is in such chaos at the moment is that Carol really can't decide what she wants to do. Dave can't wait to retire because he has a full life outside of the business. He loves playing golf, and he wants to be out on the course every day. He's annoyed that he still has to spend some of his days at work. This is why he's so tired of the family business drama. The sooner he can wash his hands of the company, the better, so far as he's concerned.

Carol, on the other hand, doesn't have a lot of interests outside of the office. Besides designing her own future home (a short-term project once she has the time), the only other thing she does with her time is hang out with her kids. But she does that at work as well. She knows she's getting older, her husband wants to retire, and it's probably the right time to start handing responsibilities over to her kids, but there's nothing for her to look forward to on the other side. So she clings to various roles, even though she's exhausted and knows she needs to slow down.

This has left her half in and half out of the company. And that's not good for her, her family, or the business. For the succession process to work, for her children to take over, and for the company to survive, she needs to learn to step away—and to relearn how to live her own life.

A LACK OF LIFE KILLS

If all you have is business, you have nothing to build a life on when the business goes away. This can be dangerous for your relationships. If the only way you connect to family is through work, what do you do when work is over? And what do you do if things are going poorly in the office? What do you do if you have to let a member of the family go? The risks here are significant.

And living to work isn't just a risk for your relationships either. If you only exist for your job, as soon as the job is gone, you may lose all sense of purpose. You may struggle to find a reason to live. And that literally can kill you.

There have been numerous studies that show how dangerous it is to live a life without some sense of work and purpose. I saw this play out firsthand with my father-in-law. He was a healthy, strong man. But as soon as he retired, he started deteriorating. I watched him spend his last few years sitting around, watching old westerns. Seemingly overnight, he wasted away.

So unless you intend to stay in your job up to the day you die, you need to start working to live instead of living to work.

CREATE A LIFE PLAN

To avoid that fate, you need to begin filling your life with more life. And to do that, you should ask yourself a fundamental question: what are you going to do *after*?

What are you going to do after work today? What are you going to do after this workweek? What are you going to do after you retire?

If you want to live a rich life, you have to build a life plan around the six Fs:

- Foundation
- Fitness
- Finances
- Family
- Friends
- Faith

Everything falls into these categories. Most of them are fairly self-explanatory. However, it's worth adding some additional clarity on a few of them. For instance, foundation refers to developing yourself. Learn a new language, take up tennis, plan a road trip: whatever adds new value to you, pursue it. Fitness, meanwhile, includes exercise but also diet and mental health. And family refers not just to your spouse and children but more distant relations. Under finance, we can find not just having enough in the bank but the charities you donate to.

We all have weaknesses in this list. No life is perfect, but the aim is to build all of these up so that you have a rich living experience beyond the office walls.

In every family council, I always ask four questions:

- What's going well?
- What's not going well?
- What are we learning?
- What should we do differently?

We can ask those same questions here. Which of the six Fs are going well for you? Which are not going well? What are you learning from those successes and failures? What can you do differently to improve in the areas you're weakest? For me, I'm very strong on my foundations, friends, finance, and faith. But I could do more on some family relationships. I have a brother I would like to be closer to. And so I make a point to reach out to him regularly—to maintain that contact. After my gallbladder surgery last year, I'm putting more time into fitness as well.

To make clear improvement, you can also put each of these categories on a scale. From one to ten, where are you in each of the six Fs right now? What needs to happen to get one or two points closer to ten over the next year in each category?

Again, you don't have to aim for perfection. Just a little bit better is much better than before.

If we attend to these areas of our lives, we naturally build a life that is more than our business. The more we focus on building our lives, the more life there is beyond the office. And that can only be a good thing.

ARE YOU READY TO MOVE ON?

Having your life plan in place makes the option of retirement more realistic. It can make it feel less like a decision you dread and more like one you look forward to. Additionally, following all the advice in this book can create the circumstances for you to step away from the business whenever you feel it's right without fearing the whole company will come crumbling down.

But having all that in place doesn't mean it's the right moment to retire yet. Retirement for you might be this year, but it might be in a decade. To get a clearer idea when retirement is the right choice for you, I recommend you take the Value Builder assessment. There's also a lot of great advice in Bob Buford's book *Halftime*.

Even if you feel like you're many years away from this decision, there's no reason to put off getting clarity on when would be a good time to focus on living for the rest of your life. In fact, just like with so much advice in this book, it's always better to start working on this now. You never know if an unexpected event will push your timeline to retire closer than you expected. And you never know how much you might be missing out on by putting off your life plan until later.

I don't know how many times I've spoken to founders who have finally stepped away from their company and realized how much they've missed out on in life. They waited until they were older and tired before they realized how much they loved to travel or how much they enjoyed volunteering. I speak from personal experience here. One of the most valuable things I do with my time is volunteer. It's enriched me more than any day in the office ever has. I wouldn't trade that time for anything.

So even if you aren't near retirement, take the opportunities now to live beyond the office. According to author and entrepreneur Alan Weiss, "Real wealth is measured in discretionary time."

If you don't have a lot of discretionary time, you aren't wealthy, no matter how much money you have in the bank. You can always earn more money in your business; you can't get any more time.

Take this moment to enjoy all the time you have left. Find a new hobby, reconnect with an old friend, volunteer at a local charity, start training for that mini-marathon. You won't regret it.

IT'S ALL ABOUT FAMILY

As you focus on building up your life plan, there's one obvious area to turn your attention to first: your family. After all, that's what this is all about, right? You want peace in the home and prosperity in the business. As you start seeing more of that prosperity through the tools we've covered in this book and transfer some of it to increased discretionary time, don't forget to invest that time with family. Even if you see them every day in the office, there's no better way to spend your free hours than with the people you love most.

And that means spending time with family that has nothing to do with business at all. I'm as guilty of blurring the lines of family business as everyone else. I remember one conversation with my daughter, Staci, a couple years ago. I'd been going on at length about business strategies when she pulled me up short.

"Stop coaching, Dad. Can't we just talk about the Cowboys?"

She was absolutely right. I'd gotten so in the habit of helping her build our family business, I'd forgotten how to have a normal conversation with her. So we put business aside for the day, and we talked about football.

Those business-free days have become a real delight for me—so much so that I now make it a priority to plan for them ahead of time. For Staci's birthday, for instance, I took her, my wife, and myself out to get mani-pedis and drink margaritas.

Not once did we talk about business.

As evening approached on a wonderful afternoon, Staci said, "This is the best day I've had in months."

All I could do was smile.

That's what it's all about.

CONCLUSION

MY CLIENTS CALL ME IN TO COACH THEM FOR ONE OF TWO reasons: inspiration or desperation. Inspiration cases involve family businesses hoping to take things to the next level. They need a little help with some of the basics like strategy or financial literacy, and once they master that, the world is theirs to conquer. Desperation cases involve those family businesses that have already let things go pretty wrong, and they're hoping I can help them salvage their business and their family.

I've shared a lot of desperation cases in this book. For obvious reasons, though, I prefer the kind of stories I didn't need to tell in this book: the inspirational clients who mostly have these ideas in place already. With them, we set some ambitious targets, and we plot the way to get there. It's very fulfilling and far less stressful. Everything is easier when you're already winning.

But I still care about those desperation cases. Nothing is worse than fearing the loss of your family or your business. While it's fun working for the inspirational clients, helping save a desperate founder is the most rewarding work I do.

So, whether you've read this book for inspiration or desperation, I hope there's been much that can help you here. More than anything, I hope this book inspires you to take these steps now so you don't have to call me later. I hope you can avoid reaching the point some of the founders were at in this book.

To take those first steps and avoid the worst possible fate for your family and business, choose the area where you feel you're weakest—whether it's a business practice or a family strategy—and start working right away. As you implement changes, they can build, strengthening every aspect of family, business, and life. They can reduce stress, increase productivity, remove the risk of unnecessary disagreements and miscommunication, and provide everyone with a role they can own.

You don't have to do this on your own. I have a free family business assessment you can take at www.familyceos.com. And if you need further guidance, you can reach out to me at mike@familyceos.com.

Before you know it, you may find that you aren't so desperate anymore—that you really can have peace in the home and prosperity in the office.

ACKNOWLEDGMENTS

I WANT TO THANK MY WIFE, TAMMY, WHO ALLOWED ME TO pursue my dream of owning my own business and helping others. You are my partner, soulmate, and best friend.

Also a huge thank-you to my daughter, Staci, who provides a living lab of what works and does not work in a family business. She has blossomed into a strong leader and entrepreneur.

Thanks to my coaches and colleagues who have provided support, encouragement, and the occasional butt-kicking I needed along this journey. Thank you, David Herdlinger, who got me started on this crazy coaching ride. Thank you, Bill Napolitano, my coach, my friend, and one of the best examples of how to do it right. Thank you, Doug Brown, for teaching me how to sell. Thank you, Keith Cupp, who helped me see a bigger future for myself and others. Keith, you are an inspiration to me. Thank you to Shannon Susko, for setting an example of how to learn and grow as a coach and allowing me to be a part of your amazing work. Thank you, Ken Stiles, for the spiritual encouragement I needed.

I would be remiss if I didn't thank my clients, who over the last twenty-four years have taught me so much about how to run a successful business, as well as how to have a life to go with it. I am eternally grateful to them for allowing me to be a part of their journey to having the business and life they want.

I would also like to thank my friends and former colleagues at Interstate Batteries. I would not be here if they had not given me an opportunity to ride the roller coaster with them. My mentors, Len Ruby, Carlos Sepulveda, Norm Miller, and Tommy Miller, taught me how to treat people, develop deep relationships, and reach for the stars. I will forever be grateful for your support and encouragement.

To my "council" of friends, my guys who are my sounding board—Michael Ryer, Blake Cooper, Randy Starks, B.J. Stephenson, and Scott Congdon—you guys have supported me all along the way, and I cherish your friendship and council along the way.

Finally, to our team at ProActive. Darren, Julie, Nancy, and Bill, you guys challenge me, inspire me, and help me laugh along the way. I could not do this without you.

ABOUT THE AUTHOR

AS THE FOUNDER OF THE PROACTIVE LEADERSHIP GROUP, Michael (Mike) Mirau strives to empower and inspire business leaders to achieve the greatness that lies within themselves and their organizations in order to ultimately fulfill their purpose with passion and excellence.

His experience working with senior executives in large corporations, as well as small businesses, brings a unique combination of perspective, experience, and education to help his clients get improved results and performance personally and with their organizations.

Mike provides business coaching and consulting to middle-market companies and nonprofit organizations. His coaching helps organizations get healthy and become scalable. The ProActive Strategic Excellence process transforms organizations and helps them focus on the things they need to do to take their business to the next level. His coaching style, passion, commitment, and skill allow business owners to experience the results they are seeking.

Over the last twenty years, Mike has worked with more than

a thousand different companies in a hundred different industries. His background in technology, healthcare, wholesale distribution retail, and family businesses has helped companies drive team engagement and dramatically improve revenues and profits. As a certified coach in multiple methodologies, Mike utilizes the latest tools and technologies to help clients chart their path and then holds them accountable to execute their plans.

Mike's previous careers include senior executive and information systems management responsibilities in several different companies, including E-Systems, JCPenney, and Interstate Batteries. He also helped start a successful internet company that was sold to News Corp in 2001. Mike is also the founder and CEO of Tribute Printing Solutions, a specialty printing company headquartered in Mesquite, Texas.

Made in the USA
Columbia, SC
02 October 2024

42876674R00107